SALT & LIGHT

SALT & LIGHT

Inspirational Stories of Faith at Work

Published by Marshall Cavendish Editions
An imprint of Marshall Cavendish International

Other Marshall Cavendish Offices:
Marshall Cavendish Corporation, 800 Westchester Ave, Suite N-641, Rye Brook, NY 10573, USA • Marshall Cavendish International (Thailand) Co Ltd, 253 Asoke, 16th Floor, Sukhumvit 21 Road, Klongtoey Nua, Wattana, Bangkok 10110, Thailand • Marshall Cavendish (Malaysia) Sdn Bhd, Times Subang, Lot 46, Subang Hi-Tech Industrial Park, Batu Tiga, 40000 Shah Alam, Selangor Darul Ehsan, Malaysia

National Library Board, Singapore Cataloguing in Publication Data

Names: Salt&Light Private Limited.
Title: Salt & light : inspirational stories of faith at work.
Description: Singapore : Marshall Cavendish Editions, [2021] | "Salt&Light Private Limited"—Title page verso.
Identifiers: OCN 1201221543 | ISBN 978-981-4893-71-8 (paperback)
Subjects: LCSH: Work—Religious aspects—Christianity. | Religion in the workplace. | Employees—Religious life.
Classification: DDC 248.88—dc23

Printed in Singapore

Contents

Leadership

Faith

Work

Foreword

"To glorify God in the digital space.
"To transform the marketplace, one story at a time.
"To exhort, encourage, equip Christians to put God first in their lives through digital discipleship."

This is the vision of *Salt&Light*.

I am so glad that you are reading this book! If any of these stories speak to you then it will be the best reward for the entire *Salt&Light* team and the people who supported it.

We thank God for His provision and guidance for *Salt&Light*. Since the launch of the website in January 2018, so many people have contributed with their stories from the marketplace. Some are inspirational, some are touching and yet others are useful tips for the marketplace. But one thing they have in common: God is front and centre in every story.

Imagine the challenge for the editorial team to pick the stories to be published in this book. "So many good stories and so little space."

We are all sojourners in the world. As we journey together in faith, I hope this book will be a blessing to you no matter what circumstances you face at work or in life. And my prayer for you is taken from Numbers 6:24-26: "The Lord bless you and keep you; the Lord make his face shine on you and be gracious to you; the Lord turn his face towards you and give you peace."

Lastly, may I encourage you to go M.A.D (**M**ake **A** **D**ifference) in wherever God places you and transform the marketplace.

To God be the glory!

Lucas Chow

Introduction

We have a disconnect.

The faith that Christians in Singapore profess around our neck isn't always a faith that can be discerned through our mouths or our hands – especially when it comes to a faith lived out at the workplace.

One of the joys of living in a multi-racial, multi-religious country is the fact that, because we rarely face persecution for our faith, most Christians feel no need to hide their religious allegiance.

In a National Survey of Christians in the Marketplace (*https://saltandlight.sg/marketplace-survey/*) conducted as a precursor to *Salt&Light*, 91.3% of respondents said "most people at work know I'm Christian".

In the demographically-representative survey of 2,000 Christians (Protestant and Catholic) in Singapore conducted between 2016 and 2018, only 13.7% of respondents said they keep their religious beliefs private at work. On the surface, that's hugely encouraging. That means that 86.3% – more than 6 in 7! – are open to their colleagues knowing that they are Christian.

In fact, 91.1% said daily life would be "meaningless" without a sense of spirituality. Even more, 94.2%, said they "agree" or "strongly agree" that their faith has a "considerable influence" over all aspects of their life.

So, clearly, Christians in Singapore know that their faith should inform all of their life, all of the time. Yet when asked about how this is specifically lived out in their lives, the answers in the survey don't seem to match the big-picture convictions.

For example, when asked how often they try to apply biblical principles on values and ethics at work, 49.8% of those surveyed responded that they never did so, or only did so rarely/sometimes. That's a far cry from the 9 in 10 we saw earlier.

Under a quarter of respondents – 22.3% – declared they were "purpose-driven Christians living out their calling in the workplace". The remaining 77.7% said they could see God starting to use them, or know their call but aren't living it out, or struggle to see how God could use them there.

In other words: Most Christians don't fully see why God put them where they work.

Asked about a few other faith-related activities, only about a third said they have items at their workplace to remind them of their faith; publicise Christian events or materials at work; or meet other Christians at work to pray.

None of these acts, of course, is in itself an absolute indicator of a faith fully lived out. But taken as a whole, it paints a picture that maybe there's still some way to go in how often we as Christians bring Christ with us to the workplace.

"While faith remains very important for marketplace Christians in Singapore, only a fifth feel that they are fully living out their calling at the workplace," surmises the author of the survey.

So, we have a disconnect between the theory and the reality of faith at work. But you didn't need a survey to tell you all that. You know it's true because if it were you doing the survey, maybe you'd struggle to call yourself truly purpose-driven every day at your cubicle.

You know it's true because at your cell group, when you get to the bit where you share about your life and its struggles, so much of the conversation is dominated by issues to do with colleagues, salaries and workplace ethics.

You know it's true because of the times you've found yourself thinking at work: I can't believe that guy is a Christian. And then wondering if others have thought the same about you, too.

Don't feel bad if that describes you. The point isn't self-condemnation, self-flagellation. The Bible is clear: We don't see the reality of our situation just so we can be resigned to it. We take pause, take stock, then take action – appropriate steps to ensure we're doing things God's way.

But how does it look to work God's way?

The truth is that faith and work aren't meant to be separate, competing realms. Work is meant to be a subset of faith, not a competing demand.

"You are not your own; you were bought at a price. Therefore honour God with your bodies." (1 Corinthians 6:19-20)

"Whatever you do, work at it with all your heart, as working for the Lord, not for human masters." (Colossians 3:23)

Our work is meant to be all His. This is true even if we don't know or want it to be true; it applies even before we surrender it to Him.

In other words, if we do it His way, He gets all the glory, and we reap all the rewards of obedience. But if we choose to go our own way – to hold some back for ourselves – then the consequences set out by His Word and laws apply because this realm is all His.

"Many are the plans in a man's heart, but in the end the Lord's purpose prevails." (Proverbs 19:21)

And this explains one last sobering set of statistics I'll quote you from the National Survey on Christians in the Marketplace.

Only 49.7% of Christians say they often sense God's presence while at work. That means more than half don't. Similarly, 49.8% say they do not often see the connection between their worship and their work.

And 43.1%, say they never, rarely, or only sometimes view their work as a partnership with God.

All of which suggest that this is the current state of Christendom in the Singaporean office: Often there without the presence of God. Often unworshipful. And often not in partnership with God – a shame, because He put us where we are in the first place.

That's the disconnect: We're here for a reason, but we lose sight of that amid the busyness of business.

How are we supposed to be a good and godly worker and spouse and parent and child and ministry worker and cell member all at once?

It's impossible to answer that question in this one article, or even in one book – which is why we launched the website https://saltandlight.sg in January 2018.

In this website, every day, we publish stories, devotionals and videos that exhort, encourage and equip believers to live out our faith at work.

This book you now read is a compilation of some of the most inspiring stories that have been published in our first couple of years in existence. We believe the testimony of the saints (Revelation 12:11) should be our natural and intentional response to the goodness of God – to be *Salt* that preserves and flavours the Earth, and *Light* that illuminates a world shrouded in darkness.

Salt&Light is named after Matthew 5:13-16, the famous passage from Jesus' Sermon on the Mount.

Should salt lose its saltiness, Jesus said, it's only good to be thrown out. And why be given a light only to put it under a bowl?

We believe it's time for the light in us to be uncovered, that it pours forth into every realm of darkness around us, particularly where we spend the majority of our waking hours – at the workplace.

We believe it's time for Christians to arise and act out our collective and individual kingdom purposes, wherever we are placed.

We believe it's time to address the disconnect. So that we don't keep our faith and work as separate, occasionally overlapping realms, but intentionally bring Jesus with us to work – and acknowledge that He is Lord there, too.

Edric Sng
Editor, *Salt&Light*

Leadership

Meekness in leadership? It's possible, says Choe Peng Sum in farewell look-back at Frasers Hospitality

Choe Peng Sum was the first employee of Frasers Hospitality. He left and joined Pan Pacific Hotels Group as CEO in September 2019. All pictures courtesy of Frasers Hospitality.

Within the hospitality industry, Choe Peng Sum is regarded as the stalwart who built Frasers Hospitality.

After leading the company for more than 20 years, Choe announced his retirement as chief executive in February, but he remains an advisor to Frasers Property.

The 59-year-old leaves a track record of having developed Frasers Hospitality into a global brand, with a chain of 150

"I'm very proud of Frasers' high performing teams all over the world. Many of the general managers started out as front office managers," says Choe. Fraser Suites, Shenzhen, 2018.

properties spread across 80 cities worldwide. It is a record that is hard to beat.

But more than the awards and accolades, it is his staff's regard of him as a *workplace minister* that Choe holds dear.

Salt&Light sat down with the doyen of the hospitality industry to talk about the faith he brought to his role.

WHAT DOES IT MEAN TO BE A WORKPLACE MINISTER?

On my birthdays, the staff would give me these huge cards, where everyone writes a greeting. One birthday, a staff member wrote: "Happy Birthday! Thank you so much, you are a pastor to us in the workplace."

I read it and just stood there for a while, then I whispered: "Lord, thank you so much."

You can be a pastor in church, but you can also be a pastor in the workplace.

"God brings us to our workplace so that we can influence the environment."

In another incident, God told me to speak to this colleague. I didn't know why but I went over and asked how he was.

He's in sales and marketing, a very cheerful guy and a fellow believer. He said: "Yeah, yeah, all's good."

I persisted, asked about the family and again if everything was alright. That's when he broke down; his daughter had been diagnosed with cancer.

God brought his name up so that we could pray. That's what the workplace ministry is about.

WHAT IS THE RELEVANCE OF FAITH AT WORK?

God is very relevant. We can bring our work before Him because the ongoing relationship with Him is so important.

As you go through new experiences, and with more responsibilities, it's great to commune and pray.

Philippians 4:6-7 says: "Do not be anxious about anything, but in everything by prayer and supplication, with thanksgiving, let your requests be made known to God. And the peace of God, which surpasses all understanding shall keep your hearts and your minds in Christ Jesus."

"Many times at work, it's how we behave, how we react in difficult situations, that will convince someone that God is alive," Choe shares. Celebrating Fraser Suites Beijing's 10th anniversary with his staff in 2018.

When I look back in my journal, I am wow-ed to see God's hand in every decision, difficulty and crossroad. That's how relevant He is.

CAN YOU GIVE AN EXAMPLE OF HOW PHILIPPIANS 4:6-7 CAME THROUGH FOR YOU?

We were intending to buy a property in Beijing at a time when the market was overheating.

The Beijing authorities wouldn't allow foreign investments then and required any property purchase of over US$100 million to be made through Beijing.

We met with the best consultants and our lawyers. After major deliberations, the consultants suggested that we list the purchase in Tianjin instead. (Tianjin borders Beijing municipality). They also advised us to break up our purchase of the mixed-development property into two separate deals – buying the shopping mall and the hotel separately. That way, each property would be below the US$100 million price tag.

Everyone in the room thought it was a brilliant idea but I had an uncomfortable feeling about it.

I excused myself and found a quiet cubicle to pray. When I got the answer, I went back to the meeting.

> "What we need to know in business is in the Word of God."

I told the team we would list the purchase in Beijing. And we would purchase the property as a whole unit and will not break it up into two.

The expressions on the consultants' faces read: "He's going to lose this deal." You could tell they were rolling their eyes in their hearts.

A little after six months, we got the news that the purchase was approved.

But more than that, a year later, the authorities clamped down hard on those who had bought properties in Beijing but listed them elsewhere. They were fined and had to pay back taxes as well.

"The testimony about Kingdom values – that's all I carry with me," Choe states. With his team at the Business Traveller China Awards, 2015.

If I had listened to the consultants, I would have had to pay many millions in back taxes.

Some may say this is pure coincidence. But it's never a coincidence. God is in control. He doesn't say pray to me only about the big things, but *anything and everything, by prayer and supplication*.

HOW DO YOU BRING CHRISTIAN PRINCIPLES INTO YOUR MANAGEMENT?

A lot of what we need to know in business is in the Word of God. He brings us to our workplace so that we can influence the environment.

"Christians should not just flow along but make a positive influence at work."

When I was still at school, the Lord had asked me: "What kind of boss do you want? One who always scolds, breathes down your neck and constantly tells you what to do? Or a boss who trusts, encourages and helps develop you?"

I said: "Lord, definitely a boss who encourages and looks at my positives rather than my negatives."

So, when I lead, I try to see the positives and encourage. This is the Golden Rule that Jesus spoke of: "So whatever you wish that others would do to you, do also to them, for this is the Law and the Prophets." (Matthew 7:12)

"For me, one of my callings was to expand the business into various countries, where it's easier for tentmakers to go," says Choe. At the Fraser Residence Menteng grand opening, 2014.

Frankly speaking, you can always find fault and focus on the negatives and breathe down necks. Or you can choose to look at your staff's positive points and build them up.

When you hire the right people and empower them, they will take the initiative and can come up with even better ideas.

"We have to drive results, we need to move, but we don't have to make people suffer for that."

As a leader, I need to give clear directions and set clear goals.

If the staff makes errors, I have to provide an environment for them to try, fail, and then try again.

This is the difference Christians can make – to be a positive influence, not just flow along, but to make a difference in the work environment.

"The greatest joy as a leader is to be able to influence the environment," says Choe at the Influential Brands Award in 2016.

Where a Christian leader is, that's where God should be present.

WHAT DO YOU THINK IS GOD'S PURPOSE FOR CHRISTIANS IN LEADERSHIP?

I think it's a calling that God will make clear to each individual.

Christian leadership is to influence the atmosphere and to allow the freedom of worship. God has put Christians in leadership to make certain decisions; we need to step up and take responsibility.

Leaders can lead based on biblical principles to create a different atmosphere.

For example, Matthew 5:5 says the meek shall inherit the earth but the world says the aggressive, the assertive, or the powerful will inherit the earth. No one except God will say the meek, the humble, will inherit the earth.

If we can be that, we have influenced the environment. We have used Kingdom principles that are opposite to the world's wisdom. God uses the foolish to shame the wise (1 Corinthians 1:27-29). And if we work in His power, people can tell.

WHILE WE MAY WANT TO BE MEEK, OUR BOSSES MAY WANT US TO BE MORE AGGRESSIVE. HOW DO WE STAND UP TO THAT?

I believe that God will bring results.

Meekness is not about having low standards.
We need excellence. (1 Corinthians 10:31)

Results are more powerful than words. I have seen that when God gives the calling to lead, He will also provide the grace.

Now, having said that, meekness is not about having low standards. We need excellence.

1 Corinthians 10:31 says: "In whatever we do, whether we eat or drink, we do it all to the glory of God."

God will give the grace to be a servant leader, to be meek and yet produce results. At the end, everyone will know it's not you, it's God.

God will make a way. When others see, they will say God's hand is with you. I think that is the testimony we can have.

Choe asked God: "How can I influence 150 properties in 80 cities, worldwide with the same culture based on Kingdom values?" With his management team at the GM Forum, 2018.

WHERE DO YOU GET YOUR INSPIRATION AND BUSINESS STRATEGIES TO LEAD THE COMPANY?

It comes from spending time with God.

When I face issues at work, I take half a day's leave. I bring my notebook and spend time with God in the outdoors. I'll read the Bible and have conversations with the Lord. Most times it's not an audible voice but you get a sensing (Jeremiah 29:13).

We tend to be so busy and get caught up with work. But if we take time, God is there for us. I'm not saying that God is an ATM (automated teller machine), but sometimes what we do not have is because of what we do not ask.

DOES GOD ALSO POINT OUT WHEN YOU ARE ON THE WRONG TRACK?

Many, many times. We were planning to list the REIT (Real Estate Investment Trust) and I was pressing the people because of deadlines.

> No one except God will say the meek, the humble, will inherit the earth. If we can be that, we have influenced the environment.

One morning, while doing my quiet time, God reprimanded me from Proverbs 27:23. God spoke to me: "Know well the condition of your flocks, and give attention to your herds."

I took that to mean the condition of my staff, and I felt God asking if I knew how they were.

That morning, I called them in, one by one.

They had all been working hard without complaint. But as I talked to them, the tears just flowed because of the pressure they were facing.

I realised I was driving my team too hard. It also showed that God's heart is for the people, not just the believers. Christian leaders are put into position to look after our flocks.

That taught me a big lesson: We have to drive results, we need to move, but we don't have to make people suffer for that.

YOU LAUNCHED FRASERS HOSPITALITY TRUST, THE FIRST GLOBAL HOTEL AND SERVICED RESIDENCE TRUST TO BE LISTED ON THE SGX. WAS THAT A GOD IDEA?

Our team was working towards the listing when the bank president flew in from London to meet with us. And he tells us: "It's not the right time to list and if any other banks tell you to do so, they are lying."

He then went on to present many charts that showed a weakened economy.

After the bankers left, we just sat. What do we do now? I told my team: "I don't know what to do but I think we should just fast and pray."

Around the table, they all agreed. Even the non-Christians were saying: "Ya, ya, I think we better fast and pray." Sometimes I think it's okay to be honest.

After a few days, the whole team met again and they unanimously agreed: "Let's do it!"

When we listed in 2014, we were 21 times oversubscribed.

It's definitely God, it's not us.

◆Text by Karen Tan

"I'm really proud of our miracle nation": NVPC's Melissa Kwee on her dreams for a City of Good

Melissa Kwee has headed the National Volunteer and Philanthropy Centre (NVPC) since 2014.
Picture by Tan Huey Ying

Melissa Kwee is a scion of the Pontiac Land Group family, real estate developers and owners of luxury hotels such as the Capella Singapore, famous for being the location of the historic Trump-Kim Summit in June 2018.

Yet instead of opting for a life of glitz and glamour, Kwee has chosen to give her time and efforts back to the community.

Kwee is the CEO of the National Volunteer and Philanthropy Centre (NVPC), a non-profit organisation promoting a giving culture in Singapore in an effort to build a City of Good.

This is not her first role in community work. Melissa had plunged straight into social entrepreneurship right after university.

The anthropology graduate from Harvard University was awarded the Singapore Youth Award in 2007 and ASEAN Youth Award 2008 for her leadership and service in that sector.

Salt&Light sat down with Kwee to hear her vision of Singapore as a City of Good.

YOU HAVE BEEN IN PHILANTHROPY FOR MORE THAN TWO DECADES – WHERE DO YOU GET YOUR INSPIRATION?

Growing up, I saw my maternal grandparents being very engaged in community always, and eventually making the decision to give pretty much all their wealth to the community.

The school I went to also had a real emphasis on raising citizens who are socially conscious, environmentally aware and politically engaged.

The people I meet also inspire me. I try and hold, front and centre, the idea that you can learn something from anyone if you are open and curious.

I'm more of a spontaneous, go-with-the-flow type of person. I just trust that, if you're really asking God to show you His will, and if you want to be in God's will, then you just have to keep moving.

In 2018, Melissa Kwee was appointed a Justice of the Peace.

And until doors start closing, or things start falling apart, or when you have the conviction that you are walking down the wrong path, you just keep tuning in.

As a child of God, it is also important for me to be a peacemaker (Matthew 5:9).

To help teenage girls on probation reintegrate into society, Melissa Kwee co-founded Beautiful People, initially a ground-up programme of Beyond Social Services, which pairs mentors with teenage girls to offer guidance, life skills and friendship. This has become more than a volunteer role for her, this is now family.

OVER THE YEARS, HAVE YOU SEEN SINGAPOREANS BECOME BETTER AT GIVING?

Giving has changed because of demographics and changing life experiences.

There is a strong wave of millennials who are looking for causes to get behind and for ways to make a difference. They see the different problems in society and want to do something about it. Many want to work for companies that do good; others want to start social enterprises.

You also see a demographic shift with the first generation of older adults who are educated, aware and have leisure time, want to be relevant and make a contribution,

We're also more globally connected and people are more aware of big issues like climate change – and people seeking to make a difference with small lifestyle changes. Small things ultimately add up. We are also talking more about taboo issues like mental health and social isolation. It can happen to anyone of us.

WHEN WE THINK OF SINGAPOREANS, A GIVING PEOPLE DOES NOT COME TO MIND. WHAT DO YOU THINK?

That's why we have to articulate an alternative narrative, to have a different definition of who we are as a people!

Giving is defined, not just as the act of volunteering or the sharing, but *who we are*. It is also about having a spirit of being other-centred.

So at NVPC, we have a goal to establish the identity of Singaporeans as a giving people, as a giving nation, where goodness is part of who we are.

A "city of good" narrative is where people, organisations, businesses as well as leaders come together to give their best for others.

HOW FAR ARE WE FROM BECOMING A CITY OF GOOD?

In my mind, I use the Kingdom of God as the dynamic – because it is in you, it is coming, it is now. It's beyond time and space but it is accessible to everyone.

The whole point is for each person to discover that gift and talent within. That value within can only be realised in the giving, because things of value isn't realised unless it's given.

We try to help everyone see that it is within their realm to do good. And if it begins in the family, that's a good start. If you can extend that to your neighbour, colleagues or schoolmates, that's terrific.

In 2018, NVPC launched the SG Cares app, which makes volunteering and donating to charity easier for Singaporeans. It rides off data from giving.sg. Our dream was to make giving part of everyday life – and we clearly need platforms and partners to make that happen, said Kwee.

Many people believe that it's so hard or it requires so much commitment – but it's really just the micro movements and the habits that we cultivate every day.

WHAT DO SINGAPOREANS FIND HARDEST TO GIVE?

Time is always the most difficult to give.

I remember my dean at Harvard said he hoped we'd never become the people from whom it is easier to get $5, than five minutes of our time.

"Time is always the most difficult to give."

It's this whole scarcity-of-time perception. Time is a function of priorities. So the question is: What's your priority?

If you want companies of good, then managements need to support their employees to participate and be citizens of the community, because it will build teams and develop a sense of common cause within the company.

Purpose drives people, and people drive companies.

WHAT IS THE HARDEST PART OF YOUR JOB?

I believe that human beings ultimately want to do the right thing. Nobody sets out wanting to be selfish or evil. Everybody wants to do good and be proud of what they do.

But we also operate in a system that tends to be quite win-lose and very harsh on failure. The perception of failure is to receive judgement.

The sense of failing or losing out is such a strong cultural belief that it often causes people to become selfish, territorial, judgmental and self-righteous.

When people don't put the welfare of others first, when they don't take a step back and see what is the common good but pursue exclusively a narrow private interest, that's ultimately where things fall apart.

A group of Singapore filmmakers and online creators produced 15 short films based on real-life Singaporean stories from the early 1970s to the late 1990s.

Melissa Kwee with Daniel Yun (Blue3Asia) at Filmgarde Cineplexes. *15 Shorts* was a collaboration between NVPC and Blue3Asia. Early in her career, Melissa Kwee started Project Access, a values-based leadership education initiative to inspire and equip girls and young women to be role models for positive change.

SO HOW DO YOU OVERCOME THAT?

First of all, I always think we have the choice to love or judge.

In facing selfishness, I believe it starts by having the opposite spirit, and modelling a generosity of spirit.

It is not about cursing the darkness but lighting a light.

For example, *15 Shorts*, a collaboration between the National Volunteer & Philanthropy Centre (NVPC) and Blue3Asia, features real people's stories told through short films.

What's strategic? It's the focus on local Singaporeans. That helps to expand our understanding of Singapore's social history.

Otherwise, Singapore's history is either told in an economic sense or political self-determination perspective. It's not told as a people's history.

"It is not about cursing the darkness but lighting a light."

Creatives today are our prophets – they shape the public mindset and cast attention on what can be achieved through caring and sacrificing for others.

We want to use content to stimulate positive action, so after watching the clips online, viewers can also click through to giving.sg, to connect to a cause and make a difference.

PEOPLE CAN GET DULL OF HEARING THE CALL TO GIVE AND VOLUNTEER – HOW DO YOU PREVENT THIS COMPASSION FATIGUE?

I think I'm wiser now to discern what programmes are more likely to have impact, and what is just a lot of activity with nice packaging.

For young people especially, and those who are just starting out, you want to encourage them. You want to encourage their sense of purpose and wanting to be a contribution. So, I don't really ever discourage people from wanting to do that.

Sometimes, it's about managing the expectation of how much they are going to achieve and how quickly they will reach their goal. It's also about encouraging them to stay in the game rather than becoming too ambitious, and then become terribly disappointed and falling away.

I always look for people who are willing to learn, and are open-minded.

WHERE DO YOU ENVISAGE SINGAPORE IN THE NEXT 50 YEARS?

Honestly, I think Singapore is an amazing place. I'm really proud of this miracle nation.

"I think sometimes we don't dream enough."

I think sometimes we don't dream enough. We kill ideas because when we don't know how to do them, we do not spend enough time considering whether it's worth trying. Purpose, not just practicality, should be used to evaluate ideas.

Pragmatism is actually a gift, being practical helps translate things into a working model but it can become a hindrance when you limit your imagination.

The recipients of the President's Volunteerism and Philanthropy Awards 2018

If we lose our ability to dream, we lose our edge in creating a better world.

We're not perfect, but as a city, because of our level of development, investment in infrastructure and the relative stability, I think we have a potential to really accelerate urban social innovation for the benefit of all members of our community.

◆**Text by Karen Tan**

Leadership

Should we work towards success? Lucas Chow on being God's trustee

Lucas Chow's professional career spans not one but several of the biggest names in Singapore's corporate landscape, including Hewlett Packard, Singtel Mobile, Mediacorp and Far East Orchard.

So you would not be faulted for thinking his work-life must have been plain-sailing.

However, even this top honcho had moments in his career when money was scarce, balance had to be figured out, and work was drudgery.

Salt&Light spoke to him about stewardship, work-life balance and how he overcame his low points, going on to flourish in his career.

MANY ASIANS WERE BROUGHT UP TO SEE WORK AS A MEANS TO AN END; EARN YOUR MONEY TO HAVE THE LIFE YOU WANT. WHAT IS YOUR LIFE EXPERIENCE?

I grew up in a humble family and was taught to earn respect through hard work and honesty. Education was the ticket to finding a good job and getting out of poverty.

Other than earning a salary, I also invested my savings and re-invested my earnings to build up my financial portfolio. Back then, the fear of not having enough money was always on my mind.

My views on money changed when I became a Christian in my forties. I was baptised in Wesley Methodist Church and have been a member of the church ever since. John Wesley's teaching on work and money challenged me to rethink stewardship.

John Wesley preached three simple rules on money and good stewardship: Gain all you can, save all you can, give all you can.

"John Wesley's three simple rules on money and good stewardship: Gain all you can, save all you can, give all you can."

Regarding the first rule, "gain all you can", it is not wrong to work hard and make money through honest labour. It is a way to provide for yourself and family and can be put to beneficial use to help others.

1 Timothy 5:8 says: "Anyone who does not provide for their relatives, and especially for their own household, has denied the faith and is worse than an unbeliever." Therefore, making money to provide for yourself and your family is good.

However, if making money becomes an obsession and the sole reason for working, taking priority over everything else, then I think it becomes a problem.

The second rule: Save all you can. Here, Wesley talks about not spending money on things that you don't need and not to feed unnecessary desires.

I do put aside savings, so spending beyond my means is not a problem for me. But I must admit that I do "feed unnecessary desires". There is always the temptation to get that extra shirt and pants with matching shoes or get the latest phone or gadget. With online shopping and marketing promotions, buying things that I do not need has become easier!

> "Am I acting like I own the money,
> or am I acting like the Lord's trustee?"

John Wesley once asked Christians to consider this question before they spend money: Am I acting like I own the money, or am I acting like the Lord's trustee?

With God's grace, I am now more aware of how I should spend my money. I ask myself frequently John Wesley's question and consider whether I need the item or service before I make the decision to purchase.

Nevertheless, I believe God is not a killjoy! He wants to bless us with abundance so that we can have comfortable and joyful living and be a blessing to others.

The third rule is "give all you can". John Wesley provided an example of setting a budget for his annual living expenses and giving away the rest of the money he earned.

Planning for my retirement made me rethink about my income and expenses. That would be the first time in my life without a regular income. Instead, I would have to rely on God's provision.

It is the practice of our church to have an annual pledging-of-tithe exercise for planning and budgeting purposes. I recall discussing with my wife when I first retired what sum to pledge. This wasn't a problem in the past as I knew my regular income and just had to apply a 10% number to it. But with no monthly income, what was I supposed to tithe?

> "God is more generous than I ever can imagine, and He provides abundantly."

One morning in my quiet time, I was reminded that God had already provided for my retirement. Although it was not considered a regular or monthly income, He had blessed me sufficiently. Hence, I did a projection of what I expected to receive in the coming year and pledged 10% of it.

In the following months, I kept track of the money I received and tithed 10% of it. I had earlier thought my projection was too optimistic but when I totalled up my tithe giving a year later, it exceeded my earlier projection!

The lesson I learned here is that God is more generous than I ever can imagine, and He will provide for me abundantly.

I then started to set aside money for charity and other worthy causes. Although not intentional, an interesting side benefit that I got was not having to pay income tax because of the tax deduction gained from the charity giving!

From my experience, instead of spending the money on myself, using it to help others who are in need brings greater and more lasting joy. It also helps me to view my own situation in a better light. Instead of self-pity, I see how blessed I am to be in a position to give.

THERE MUST HAVE BEEN TIMES IN YOUR CAREER WHEN YOU DREADED THE WORK, HOW DID YOU OVERCOME IT?

Just like everyone else, my work is not always pleasant. Difficult colleagues and bosses, tough assignments with limited resources, feeling unfairly treated, the list goes on. In fact, there have been times when I didn't even agree with what I was asked to do!

During times like these, my first response was prayer and spending some quiet time with the Lord by reading His Word. This helped me keep things in the right perspective.

When I had to work with difficult and unfair bosses, I remind myself that God had put them as an authority over me.

Once, I had to work with a difficult colleague who had been spreading rumours about me. In my quiet time, I was reminded that God loves us regardless of how bad we are, and we, in turn, must love others. That means even if my colleague was tough to love, I had to.

God showed me His grace and reminded me that I am to follow His example to show grace to others. Besides, in that incident even if everyone believed in the false rumours and lies, God knows the truth. That gave me comfort and helped me have the right attitude when I worked with the individual.

There were other times that I had to work with bosses whom I thought were difficult and unfair. I had to remind myself that God had put them as an authority over me and I had to submit. In times like this, I would recite Colossians 3:23-24, which says: "Whatever you do, work heartily, as for the Lord and not for men, knowing that from the Lord you will receive the inheritance as your reward. You are serving the Lord Christ."

Of course, there were simply times that I just didn't feel like going to work and felt that the enthusiasm for the job had gone out the window. Then, I would pray for God's mercies and help to pull myself together so that I can deliver my work commitments and find the right motivation to continue.

I had my fair share of days when I just had to keep my head down, put my shoulder to the wheel. Putting my trust and hope in the Lord, knowing that He always wants the best for me, helped me.

HOW WOULD YOU ADVISE SOMEONE WHO IS STARTING OUT TO VIEW THE JOB OR CAREER?

Many people have asked me the question of how to have a successful career. Let's first define success. My own definition is: Success is like beauty, it's all in the eye of the beholder. You are successful when you are happy.

To be happy and successful, we need to know what we value and what are the priorities in our lives. I would suggest listing them down and reviewing them at least once a year. This is because our priorities can change with time and age.

When I had a young family, they required more of my attention and I had to set aside time for them. But now I am an empty nester, my priorities have changed.

"To me, balance is not what is in the middle. You have a balanced life when you are happy."

After knowing your priorities, check if you are allocating time to your priorities. Time is finite; we need to spend our time wisely. If spending time with your family and friends is of higher priority than work and career, you will not be very happy if you had to stay back at work, hoping to get ahead, while missing out on a family or friend's birthday gathering.

The flip side is also true: If building a career at this stage of your life is more important, you would not be very happy partying while thinking about work.

We often talk about work-life balance. To me, balance is not what is in the middle. You have a balanced life when you are happy. It will require compromises and sacrifices so that the most important things are taken care of.

No one can fit everything in. It's like a treasure box. The size is fixed, you must decide what you want to put in and what not.

◆ **Text by Karen Tan**

Leadership

What faith has to do with Singapore's $24 million Invictus Fund

The Invictus Fund is "an amazing story of God's goodness. We're talking loaves and fishes", says NCSS president Anita Fam (*left*), seen here with President Halimah Yacob (*middle*) and president of the Association of Social Workers Long Chey May (*right*). All photos courtesy of Anita Fam.

When DPM Heng Swee Keat announced in a Facebook post on June 3, 2000 that the Government would be adding $18 million to the National Council of Social Service's COVID-related Invictus Fund, the fund essentially quadrupled overnight.

The surprise announcement was met with quiet cheers from 400+ NCSS agencies with beneficiaries ranging from persons with mental health conditions to families in need.

But one woman, NCSS president Anita Fam, did more than cheer.

Ms Fam went on her knees.

She would be the first to tell you: It was not the Government who had initiated the fund. It was not NCSS, nor even she, who had initiated the fund.

It was God. And it all began with a divine download.

WHAT EXACTLY IS THE INVICTUS FUND?

The Invictus Fund essentially channels donations to social service agencies so that they can continue delivering critical care to vulnerable groups.

Except for a very small handful of critical services like family service centres, which receive 99% funding from the government and Tote Board, the majority of charities, depending on their journey or programme, might get anything from 25% to 75% of their funding from established sources. The flip side is that they have to raise 75% to 25% from public donations.

Under COVID circumstances, these charities really suffer because public donations which they rely on are drying up.

HOW WAS THE FUND CONCEIVED?

On March 27, as I was on one of my walks, I received a word from God telling me to donate $1 million to help NCSS agencies through this COVID season.

The Fund was to be the support package for our charities, as the Government did not have anything for them specifically in the earlier budgets.

"I realised that God really loves his charities."

Immediately, I went back and messaged my CEO and the designate, and said: "I'm making this donation and it's for two purposes: One is for triage for critical service providers, and the other is to support smaller charities through this COVID season. So, triage and support."

Four days later on March 31, I was on another walk when the Lord said: "Call it Invictus Fund."

I didn't even know what *invictus* meant! And I thought I'd better just go and Google to make sure it provides the right context.

And when I Googled it – "unconquered", "undefeated" – oh boy, that was the message of the Fund exactly.

I made that transfer within days of that divine instruction being given.

WERE THERE ANY FURTHER SURPRISES?

I thought I might get some friends to join in just to build up the Fund, because the bigger the Fund, the more help we could give. Internally I spoke to my Comchest chair to get his support. So I knew that there would be more than what I put in.

(Community Chest, or Comchest, is the fund-raising arm of the National Council of Social Services.)

But the quantums I was thinking of were so small. I thought we might help 50, 60 charities in a smallish sort of way, for maybe three months, to tide them over with some of their deficits.

But it started taking on a life of its own. Since we launched it probably in April, we've raised about $6.7 million for the fund.

We had corporate donations, donations from individuals. Diana Ser and friends got together to fundraise, apparently. One of the perm secs sent out an email to her colleagues sharing this as a good cause for anyone planning to donate their $600 solidarity payment.

Ms Fam (*centre*), who chairs the board of directors at Assisi Hospice, at the launch of Assisi's 50th anniversary medallion in April 2019, together with Assisi's patron, Mdm Ho Ching (*right*) and CEO Choo Shiu Ling (*left*).

Then I heard that the Government was putting $18 million into this Fund. It wasn't as if I had suggested this or actively solicited for donations. I didn't. It was mind blowing.

I realised that God really loves His charities.

DO YOU THINK THERE WAS A MESSAGE GOD WAS GIVING?
You know, with my team, the only people who knew about my donation had been my CEO, my CEO designate, the head and chairman of Comchest.

"God multiplied that $1 million into something that's $24.7 million now ... it was a divine multiplication."

And I said: "Please keep it anonymous. No one is to know." And some weeks later, after the fund had gained traction and more people were putting money into it, Minister Desmond Lee asked if he could publicly acknowledge me. And I said: "No, thank you."

The greatest fear I had was being trolled on the Internet. I don't need that.

But it's funny – in the last few weeks, I felt the Lord telling me that I needed to go public. So when my CEO called me three Fridays ago and said: "DPM wants to mention it in his Facebook post", I prayed and I said: "Lord, if you really want me to do so, I will do so in personal witness, as a testimony of Your faithfulness."

By that time, you know, there was this amazing story of God's goodness. We're talking loaves and fishes, because He multiplied that $1 million into something that's $24.7 million now.

And that is the message: God brought about a divine multiplication. It's got nothing to do with me. My act in it was just a simple act of short-sighted obedience.

AT YOUR PEAK YOU WERE ON THE BOARD OF 18 CHARITIES. WAS THE NCSS PRESIDENCY A NATURAL PROGRESSION FOR YOU?
Eighteen was bad – now it's not so many! I just retired from the Tote Board, so currently I have 10 appointments.

But you know, I never wanted the NCSS presidency. Never wanted it. I laid out nine fleeces* for the Lord! (**Judges 6:36-40*)

I recorded all of God's confirmations in my phone under the folder "God Notes".

At the Purple Parade 2019, a movement to include people with special needs to the main chapter of Singapore's growth, and to afford them equal access to education, employment, transport and social networks.

Finally, I received the verse Genesis 28:15: "I am with you and will watch over you wherever you go, and I will bring you back to this land. I will not leave you until I have done what I have promised you."

After that I said: "Okay *lah*, I surrender!"

When we surrender and He equips, it's got nothing to do with us anymore. It actually becomes a very liberating journey.

WHAT DO YOUR DIVINE DOWNLOADS LOOK LIKE?

Ever since I've taken on the presidency of NCSS, I have been faithfully going on walks.

I don't pray with words; it's just a time of worship. And through the years, communicating with God and hearing His voice are not unusual for me.

I used to call my route to the Asian Women's Welfare Association (AWWA) my Road to Damascus*. Whenever I was driving on that road, the Lord would tell me to do things. (**Acts 9:1-9*)

(Ms Fam is a former vice-president at AWWA.)

About 14 years ago, there was a church member who was dying of breast cancer. She had two children, a boy and a girl. I didn't know them from Adam.

But as I was driving to AWWA that day, He instructed me to ring up the church office. The Sunday before, the church had put out a call for people to help the church member. So I called up the church office and said: "I'm available to help." They said this woman's daughter, who was in Primary 6, really wanted someone to take her to Spotlight to buy things to make a friendship bracelet.

I talked to the family on the phone and took the little girl to Spotlight. I knew her mother for a grand total of six weeks before she died – I would take her to the doctors, pick her up from the hospital. The week before she died, she asked me to watch over her children. It's something I've continued to do to this day.

But it's not as if there is a download every time. Many times when I walk, I just worship the Lord. It's wonderful for the soul. And it's good exercise!

But the day that I took on the NCSS presidency – with great fear, reluctance and trepidation – I started walking even more. Because I needed to hear Him more.

HOW CAN YOU BE SURE IT'S GOD SPEAKING?

There was a missionary staying with us once – Paul Hawkins. And he would also say: The Lord told me this, the Lord told me that.

My small group would ask: "How? How did you know it's God?"

And he had this wonderful analogy: When someone close to you rings you – it may be your children or your parents – they don't have to tell you their name for you to know who it is, because there's so much familiarity. You just know.

But in order to know and recognise the voice, you need to test it in the beginning. The confirmation comes through our acts of obedience.

"I describe myself as being a Manglican – Anglican by birth, Methodist now!"

Paul Hawkins shared a story about how, one day, his wife was told by the Lord: "Go bake a lemon cake and give it to the neighbour." She thought, "That's really strange", but she did it in obedience.

She went next door and rang the doorbell, holding this lemon cake, and told the neighbour: "I baked it for you." And the young lady who opened the door burst into tears. Her husband had called her that morning and said: "I'm going to bring my boss home for dinner. And his favourite cake is lemon cake. Can you make one for him?" She didn't have any time and she couldn't bake it. And this neighbour, who was Paul's wife, had gone over and provided her with one.

In the same way, even 14, 15 years ago, every so often I would hear a voice saying donate, or send a cheque to someone. And I would do so. And then they would write back and say: Thank you so much. I really needed it at this time for such-and-such a reason.

HOW DID YOUR FAITH GET SO STRONG? WAS YOUR FAMILY A BIG FACTOR IN YOUR EARLY FAITH?

My dad and my brother did not go to church. My mum brought me to church from the time I was in kindergarten.

(Ms Fam's father is the late Michael Fam, formerly the chairman of the Housing and Development Board, and subsequently chairman of the Mass Rapid Transit Corporation and F&N.)

I was one of those kids in Sunday School who always walked away with the Sunday School prizes – Paul Tambyah and myself were always the ones. I knew him then as Ananth – we were childhood friends, Sunday School rivals!

With the family on holiday. (*L-R*) Tim, Anita, Gillian and Eck Kheng.

Raised in an Anglican church, I was confirmed when I was 13. I remember kneeling before Bishop Chiu Ban It during the confirmation. And I was wondering why he was pressing so hard on my head. But when I looked up, he wasn't even touching me. So that was my first physical encounter of the Holy Spirit.

"I realised that nothing was by chance."

It was only the following year, exactly one year to the date of my confirmation, that I really came to know the Lord. We were at a youth fellowship camp and someone had shared the four spiritual laws with me. I was just overwhelmed with remorse and burst into tears – and I'm not one to cry openly.

After that I became chairman of youth fellowship. But by the time I was 18 or 19, I stopped going to church. I was going to parties and people were making me feel guilty about going to parties and I thought it was hypocritical and I felt more and more guilty and I changed churches so no one would judge me. But when no one knows you, there's less accountability, right, so after a while I just stopped going completely.

That was like 10 years in exodus for me. It really was after I met Eck Kheng, who would become my husband, that I started going back to church again. When I was pregnant with my son, Tim, I joined a Bible study group and really started a more constant walk with God.

YOU ARE VERY OPEN ABOUT BEING ADOPTED. DID THAT HAVE AN IMPACT ON YOU?

I've known since I was about five years old that I was adopted. I was curious about the circumstances, but I never felt the urge to look for my birth mother.

Then my dad died in 2016. In 2017, my brother was cleaning up the family house when he pulled out this brown envelope that said: *Anita's documents*.

> "I've always believed that what I have materially is not mine to hoard."

He passed it to me rather awkwardly and I didn't think anything of it. That night when I opened the brown envelope, I discovered my adoption papers and my original birth certificate.

The birth cert just had the name of this 19-year-old single mum from Johor and her address was c/o Salvation Army Singapore. So she'd come to Singapore to give birth. The father's name was a dash.

And you know the most amazing thing? I looked at my adoption petition – it has to be signed by someone representing the Director of Social Welfare – and it was signed by none other than Leaena Chelliah, now Mrs Leaena Tambyah, Paul Tambyah's mum and a good friend of my mum's from church. She was the one who had invited me to join AWWA in 1994 and set me on this journey of what I am now.

Then I realised that nothing was by chance.

And, as I was holding on to my adoption papers, I heard the Lord say to me: "You are deeply favoured, My child."

And I was like: Wow. From the time I was born, He had by design orchestrated my life.

It made me even more confident that I am to do what I do in even greater obedience.

I've honestly been very blessed with the family that I've been given – in all senses. And I've always believed that what I have materially is not mine to hoard. I am to steward it, not just for my children, but others too.

That explains why, as in the Invictus Fund, when the Lord tells me to give, I give.

HOW IMPORTANT IS IT TO DISCERN THE WILL OF GOD IN OUR DECISIONS?

For Assisi Hospice, the first thing we do in our board meetings is spend time reflecting and discerning the will of God. So sometimes we reflect on a Bible passage, or a picture, for 10, 15 mins before we start our meeting.

> "The Lord doesn't just operate in the church or church boards, He's there in all that we do."

This is something that Sister Jane, the congregational leader of the FMDM sisters who started Assisi Hospice and Mt Alvernia, introduced to us. This element of discernment is what St John of God Healthcare in Australia does, and they told us what a difference it had made for their Board.

It is really about being still before the Lord, getting our hearts ready so that we are open to the Spirit's leading, rather than just being dictated by our own human actions.

And that's where I really think we need to operate more. The Lord doesn't just operate in the church, the Lord doesn't just operate on church boards, He's there in all that we do.

What I've appreciated is how God is in the "secular". I think of that wonderful example of Mr Sidkar, where God used *everyone* from different backgrounds. It didn't matter – to Him, He just loves us all.

HAS GOD EVER REMAINED SILENT WHEN YOU SOUGHT HIS COUNSEL?

Many many times. He doesn't answer immediately.

Sometimes He's answered it already but we don't recognise it because we wanted Him to answer in a certain way. Other times there's a long silence.

But it's okay. He will answer in His way and in His time.

WHICH BIBLE TENETS DO YOU LIVE BY?

I like this quote of John Wesley's a lot: "Do all the good you can, by all the means you can, in all the ways you can, in all the places you can, at the times you can, to all the people you can, as long as ever you can."

I describe myself as being a "Manglican" – Anglican by birth, Methodist now! But that quote of Wesley's really resonates.

Three Januarys ago, God also planted the seed of the Community Capability Trust Fund, a substantial sum by the Government to build up the capability of charities, to Ms Fam. Knowing that "we need very clear guidance for the social services sector", she also initiated the Government-funded Beyond COVID-19 Task Force to "take the learning from COVID and equip social service agencies to better manage themselves going forward".

And the verse that I really identify with is Jeremiah 29:11: "'For I know the plans I have for you,' declares the Lord, 'plans to prosper you and not to harm you, plans to give you hope and a future'."

That has a deep meaning for me because of my birth and story.

HAS ANY GOOD COME OUT OF COVID?

I know there are a lot of people who are suffering in terms of financial and emotional toll. My heart goes out to them.

But from my perspective, a lot of good has come out of COVID. It really is a reset button for us all. I think it's helped us appreciate time. It's helped us appreciate family. It's helped us appreciate friends.

And so, through this, I think we've realised what counts. It's not the material things.

The question is: Will we blow it by going back to the way we were? Or will we really do things differently, better?

I just pray that we come out of this valuing things and people more, not taking them for granted.

For me, I have never been more reliant on God.

◆ **Text by Juleen Shaw**

Leadership

"Singaporeans need to learn to live with mess!": 2017 Singaporean of the Year Dr Goh Wei Leong

Dr Goh Wei Leong (left) with HealthServe friends. HealthServe began when Dr Goh asked himself: "How does my faith square up with issues of poverty, exploitation, social injustice?" Photos from healthserve.org.sg.

It is Tuesday. So naturally an 8am text from Dr Goh Wei Leong reads: "G'morning from East Coast beach", swiftly followed by a picture of a quiet stretch of sand, cotton-streaked sky, ships in the distance.

This is his Tuesday morning routine: Beach, Bible, prayer, reflection. A picture of serenity.

By the time we meet for lunch, however, that solitary hour has been firmly shelved, set aside until next Tuesday.

By noon, it is time for meetings, consultations, ministry work, talks, appointments, crammed so tightly that, for this "wanted" man, a few hours spent ignoring his mobile devices subsequently means one full day replying WhatsApp messages and two days answering e-mails. And then 100 more arrive.

"This is why I don't do social media ... there is no time!" says the 2017 Straits Times Singaporean of the Year with a mock moan.

Dr Goh Wei Leong with his HealthServe team – "they do all the work, I just do the fun part, talking about it!"

He is not kidding. While Dr Goh, 59, is best known for being the chairman and co-founder of HealthServe (a medical-social enterprise serving the migrant community), he is also highly involved with Operation Mobilisation (OM) (an international, interdenominational mission organisation), Christian Medical & Dental Fellowship (CMDF) (a national, evangelical fellowship of Christian doctors and dental surgeons), and Karunya Clinic in Little India.

An involved Katong Presbyterian Church elder, he is also a seasoned speaker/moderator at forums – just last week, he moderated a panel for the newly-launched Wordly Collective, which looks at artificial intelligence in missions.

("Got to go now ... Running around today having meetings with missionary data scientists!" reads his latest intriguing text.)

All this while running his medical clinic in the notorious Jalan Kukoh area.

Ask him what he's up to, and the usual reply is: "Just one or two crazy things."

Salt&Light sat down with Singapore's Renaissance Man to find out exactly what those crazy things are and what he hopes to accomplish by them.

FIRST OFF, IS THERE A REASON YOU FAMOUSLY SHARE YOUR 2017 SINGAPOREAN OF THE YEAR TITLE WITH HEALTHSERVE?

The award came in early 2018 as HealthServe celebrated its 10th anniversary.

It's really quite wonderful that the award was given to an organisation, not an individual. It's given to a movement, a vision, a community.

We actually started HealthServe as a clinic, then added counselling services, social services, food projects, then research and advocacy – all of which are run by about 10 core fulltime staff and many volunteers, including housewives, students, doctors, lawyers.

They are the ones running it, I only do the fun part – talking about it!

WHAT DROVE YOU TO START HEALTHSERVE AND YOUR OTHER ENTERPRISES?

If I show you my original HealthServe documents – how and why it started – it really had to do with my personal faith.

I was struggling with my faith ... how does my faith square up with issues of poverty, exploitation, social injustice?

(In The Straits Times article, "Dr Goh Wei Leong switched from Maserati to charity after Mongolia trip", he talks about how, for several years, he "lost the plot" to the lure of a "good life".)

In 1995 I rediscovered Jesus when I went on a humanitarian trip to Mongolia. Life there was tough. There was a shift in my vision.

> "With me, things often start with a crazy idea. But very often the crazy idea dovetails with a need that's already there."

Later I got involved with India OM on short-term missions. As you know, India is not the easiest place, and the hardship hits you. Soon I joined OM as a regular volunteer, and ended up chairing the Board.

On a medical mission trip, a friend and I came up with the idea of starting Linking Hands, an online registry for doctors to network and form global partnerships with medical missions. So the source and the needs are matched.

I started having missions parties in my house, collecting names and data of missionaries passing through Singapore. (In those days no PDPA, so no problem!)

In 2000-2006 there was a string of disasters – the 2004 tsunami, earthquakes in Turkey, Pakistan, Iran, Palembang, Padang ... I was really busy with Linking Hands, which became a platform for aid agencies in Singapore like TOUCH International, Red Cross, World Vision. Our network grew to 65 countries.

When I was invited to run the Christian Medical & Dental Fellowship, I started sending students around the world for medical electives. I sent two to India in 2001, and within the next five years I was the medical electives guy!

Students and interns come back and become volunteers or run our programmes, so it becomes a long-term relationship.

DO YOU HAVE IDEAS PERCOLATING AT ANY ONE TIME?

With me, things often start with a crazy idea. (Laughs) But, you know what, very often the crazy idea dovetails with a need that's already there.

My friends call me a serial entrepreneur! Starting stuff is my passion. But when people ask me what I have in mind, I say: "I don't know!" I have a rough idea of what my projects will look like but I'm fine living with not knowing for sure. I think not many people can take that!

IS THERE A COMMON THREAD TO YOUR IDEAS?
Marginalised people. Bringing them into the centre of things.

IF YOU'RE A SERIAL STARTER, HOW DO YOU ENSURE THAT YOUR PROJECTS ARE SUSTAINABLE?
Young people! I cannot abide by running things with an old mindset ... buay tahan!

Young people bring in ideas that are out of the box. I'm great friends with some of them – we may be of a different age group but we are like-minded. At the get-togethers I organised, they said: "Hey I didn't know there were other people who were interested in justice, in the poor." And they started inviting their own friends. So our meetings became a very special place for like-minded people to spur one another on.

CAN YOU DESCRIBE A PROJECT THAT HAS EMBODIED THIS IDEAL?
When I was invited to chair the 34th visit of Logos Hope, OM's ship, to Singapore, I was one of the few people in Singapore at the time who thought the idea was outdated.

Yet when I was invited to chair, strangely I said yes. And I was so excited about it deep down inside, I didn't know why.

> "When I run a project, it is usually run on collective wisdom ... We share resources, wisdom, people."

I sent out an e-mail with a nice write-up calling for people to help. Twenty-three people came, HealthServe people, plus all kinds of millennials – we dubbed them the G23, as these 23 were the core group.

When I run a project, it is usually run on collective wisdom. Everybody comes together and thinks what to do, how to run it. We share resources, wisdom, people.

I accepted the role in August, the ship's visit was planned for February – a runway of just six months. I was told: "Sorry ah, the ship is coming during Chinese New Year."

I thought: "*Siao liao*. How do we do this, everything is closed."

I told the G23: "Hey guys, the ship's going to come during the first and second day of Chinese New Year."

You know what the young people said? "Hey Dr Goh, wonderful! Everything is closed during first and second day of Chinese New Year and we are open!"

And they were right. We hit a record number of visitors during the first day. The programme they came up with was so innovative – instead of "International Night" (the world is now globalised, we don't need another ethnic dance), we had breakout groups that discussed health and social justice, with Joseph Chean from YWAM as a speaker and Martin Tan from Halogen to chair the whole event. People were talking about it for a long time!

IS IT POSSIBLE FOR NEW IDEAS TO BREAK INTO TRADITIONAL SPACES, LIKE CHURCHES?

Absolutely. My church, Katong Presbyterian, had to undergo renovation. So my pastor, Rev Lam Kuo Yung, and I talked about rethinking church from scratch ... *balik* ... go back to Acts 2.

We asked ourselves: So what is church in the 21st Century? And we designed the church with input from everybody – that's the beauty of dialogue.

During the one and a half years of construction, we had different teams involved: A hospitality team, a creation care team, a creative arts team, and so forth. Our creatives art team looked into artwork for the church, and had seniors sewing art pieces.

Our creation care team got the architect to build the entire church office out of recycled church pews.

We even had a transition team, which was tasked to advise on the movement of our people during the construction. They said: We have three options; one, rent a hotel ballroom which costs about S$10,000 a month; two, rent facilities in a nearby school; three, we stay put in the construction site.

"During construction, the place was dirty and people were super inconvenienced. But we never grew more as a church."

Their proposal was to stay put. Not only would we save money, they even gave a biblical basis for it: In the Old Testament, during the Feast of Tabernacles (Leviticus 23:33-43), the Israelites lived in temporary shelters (booths) for one week, and it helped to remind them that they (and we) are all pilgrims on earth.

They said: "Let's experience some inconvenience!"

The whole committee liked this idea.

But can you imagine – during construction, we had zero carpark, the church office was in a container, and to walk to the main sanctuary, you had to pass through a narrow gap with two porta-loos. It was dirty and people were super inconvenienced.

But you know what? We never grew more as a church.

People started washing plates for each other, and saying, "Oh, you have no space for Sunday School? Here, share my space". We learnt how to share, to be other-centred, to live with mess. We made friends with the construction workers who lived on the site, knew them by name and invited them for Christmas and other meals.

And when we moved into the new sanctuary, no one complained that this or that didn't work, because we had all lived through the progress and we appreciated what we had.

My pastor started community potluck dinners with no agenda, inviting people in the neighbourhood. We needed to understand that church is very dynamic.

So our building is a reflection of our values. In July last year, 250 people moved into our church from another church. We put it to a vote – you know, Presbyterian *lah* – and 94% of our congregation said 'yes' to another church using our brand new building! Can you beat that? I was so pleased because I think the values had been absorbed.

SO DO YOU THINK SINGAPOREANS NEED TO LEARN TO LIVE WITH MESS?

Yes! Ab-so-lute-ly!

(In an interesting parallel, Dr Goh's pastor, Rev Lam Kuo Yung, writes: "The usual Singaporean ethos for running a programme is efficiency. Because we are busy and practical people, we want to get things done within the shortest time and with the smallest budget.

"Unfortunately, things done this way will only train people to be Singaporeans, not Christians.

"Running programmes for Christ requires deep reflection on our Christian ethos. Only when the organising process reflects our Biblical beliefs and values will we be spiritually formed and transformed as we work together.")

DID YOU EVER HAVE TO DEAL WITH CONFLICT?

Actually a lot of change started with a major blowout which threw the church into crisis. The crisis led us to think about what we are about, our values. Now we think that crisis was almost inevitable for our growth.

The church elders began to meet to pray because of that crisis. It's been 10 years now and every Saturday, all the elders, past and present (12-15 of us), still meet at my house for morning prayer and Bible study, followed by breakfast.

As a result of the bonding and fellowship, our monthly board meetings are a breeze!

It's a relationship framework; the transactional falls under the relational.

HOW DO THESE IDEAS ABOUT CHURCH DOVETAIL WITH YOUR ETHOS FOR SINGAPORE?

On National Day, one year before Singapore's Jubilee in 2015, I had 40 people over to my house. We asked each other: What should a Christian's response be to the Jubilee?

That was the genesis of Team Zero – "zero" because Jubilee is about resetting. How do we go back to zero? We also wanted to "zero in", be very focused about what we wanted to do.

So in the next one year, we held seven different talks on issues such as inequality, poor, migrant workers, law and justice.

One of the talks was about what God was doing among the local poor. I brought the team to Jalan Kukoh. My friend, Pastor Andrew Khoo, runs New Hope Community Services and we met at his void deck.

Dr Lai Pak Wah gave a talk about church history and poverty – right there in one of the poorest parts of Singapore – after which we had breakout groups which met at the basketball court, the HDB stairwell ... and finally we did our debrief at the empty hawker centre. It was very powerful.

Team Zero carries on now in various forms, including Micah Singapore, which champions justice issues, and Church Reform, which includes the Urban Shalom series.

DO YOU EVER HAVE DOUBTS OVER YOUR INNOVATIVE IDEAS? WHERE DO YOU GET SUCH CONVICTION?

I always start with people. My work is always collaborative, so if we fail we fail together, if we succeed, we also succeed together!

In everything I've started, I always try to be a reflective practitioner.

WHAT'S YOUR SECRET TO FITTING SO MUCH INTO 24 HOURS?

Attentive presence. However, now I'm talking to you, at the same time I'm thinking this salmon is probably farmed and we're killing the local ecosystem, and I'm noticing the baby crying at the next table ... That's the way I'm wired, I have a matrix mind but it's very *luan* (messy) *lah*!

With my life so full, I enjoy my quiet moments, like long plane rides.

DO YOU HAVE A VERSE OR BIBLE TENET YOU HOLD ON TO WHENEVER YOU LAUNCH SOMETHING?

For me, love binds everything, as John 13:34-35 says: "A new command I give you: Love one another. As I have loved you, so you must love one another. By this everyone will know that you are my disciples, if you love one another."

For my medical work, it's Jeremiah 9:23-24. God says: I don't want all these – strength and riches and talk about tithing – I'm concerned about the weighty issues, the issues of justice.

I see God working in all of these different projects.

SO GOD SURPRISES YOU?

All the time! (Laughs and slaps the table gleefully.)

◆ **Text by Juleen Shaw**

"He will bring you across the finishing line": Pastor Yang Tuck Yoong on staying the course in Christian ministry

Ps Yang, who wakes up at 4.45am every morning for prayer and devotion, says "God is more interested in meeting me than I sometimes am to meet Him. He says: 'Get up, it's time for our fellowship!'" Photo from Ps Yang's Facebook.

Remember the movie *Terminator*, when Arnold Schwarzenegger's tagline was: 'I'll be back'?

"At 60, my tagline is: 'Oh, my back!' quipped Pastor Yang Tuck Yoong.

The senior pastor of Cornerstone Community Church was speaking to the Thirst Collective team on *How to Go the Distance* in Ministry, based on wisdom gleaned from 30 years of full-time ministry.

Besides founding Cornerstone, where he cares for a flock of over 5,000 members, Pastor Yang chairs the board of Tung Ling Bible College and the annual Kingdom Invasion Conference.

At 61, he admitted wryly that he was entering a "season of diminishing returns".

"You're not as strong as you used to be. You don't have the same vitality you used to have. You take a longer time to recover from jet lag. Your bones start creaking, your skin starts sagging, your muscles start aching and your plumbing starts leaking!"

But Christian ministry is "not a short 100m sprint", he reminded.

"This is a marathon. You've got to prepare yourself mentally, spiritually and in every way."

One of the definitions of finishing well is hitting the mark that God has for us, says Ps Yang.

How then should Christians prepare themselves to persevere on this race? What does staying the course and finishing well look like?

Ps Yang shared his thoughts with *Salt&Light*:

WHAT IS A LESSON YOU LEARNED AS YOU ENTER YOUR 60S?

I had the privilege of sitting beside the late Brother Ravi Zacharias one day. We were celebrating his 70th birthday.

I had the privilege of asking him many questions and I said to him: "Brother Ravi, have you reached your sweet spot in ministry at 70 years?"

And he said to me: "You know Pastor Yang, we did a survey in America and found out that the most productive season in a person's life is 60 to 70. The second most productive season, which actually startled me, is 70 to 80. And the third most productive season in a man's life is 50 to 60.

And I said: "That's interesting", because I was just about to come into my 60s.

So I decided to check this out and found out that the average age of a Nobel Prize winner is 62. The average age of a CEO of a Fortune 500 company is 62. And the average age of the 100 biggest churches in America is between 60 to 65.

And that tells us that God has somehow designed the best years of your life when you are 60 to 70.

"We don't know when this race is going to end. The important thing is to keep your eye on the coxswain."

Growing old is like the sport of rowing. It is the only sport in which you cannot see the finishing line because when you row your back is always facing it.

But it doesn't matter. You just need to keep your eyes on the coxswain, because he can see the finishing line and you can't. *(A coxswain is the teammate who sits on the stern and faces the finishing line. He is responsible for steering the boat and coordinating the rowers.)*

Similarly, some of us might live to our 50s, some to our 70s, some to our 90s. We don't know when this race is going to end for us. The important thing is to keep your eye on the coxswain.

Hebrews 12:1-2 tells us that we are to keep our eyes on the author and finisher of our faith, Jesus Christ. And I think that's really an important part of the journey.

If you listen to His voice and keep your eyes on Him, He will bring you across the finishing line.

WHAT DOES IT MEAN TO FINISH WELL?

I recently read an interesting story about John Bisagno, a senior pastor of the First Baptist Church in Houston.

Back in his early 20s, his father-in-law, who was a senior pastor, told him that only one in 10 Christian leaders end up well in the Bible.

John couldn't believe it, but he wrote down the names of 24 of the most significant Christian leaders in his life from his city.

Growing old is mandatory but growing up is optional.

As the years went by, he periodically looked at the page he had written these names on and scratched them out one by one. Unfortunately, by the time he had gotten to 65, there were only three names left on that list.

It is staggering to realise that the majority of people do not actually finish their journey as a Christian well. Growing old is mandatory but growing up is optional.

We saw two great heroes pass away recently, Reinhard Bonnke at the end of last year (2019) and Ravi Zacharias this year (2020). When Ravi passed away, I never saw so much accolade and honour given to a man at his death.

And the reason we honour these men is that they finished well, they finished strong. They didn't mess around, they didn't play around and they didn't live at the periphery.

They were focused on what they did, they kept the fire burning and when we look at their lives, we say: "Man, this is how I want to finish."

Another definition of finishing well means hitting the mark that God has for us.

To find out the purposes for which God has created us, and to fulfil them. The Father has placed His aspirations within us, and it is our responsibility to find out what they are.

While you are young, give your life totally to God, and live your life with that perspective. Make the right choices in life.

WOULD YOU SHARE HOW REAL GOD HAS BEEN IN YOUR LIFE?

I was born again at the age of 16. This was during the Charismatic renewal. I wasn't a serious Christian. One foot in the world, one foot out of the world. One day in, one day out.

Then, I went into basic military training, and my father just died suddenly of a heart attack. When he died, I kind of tailspinned into decadence and sin.

But there was a meeting that I attended at St Andrew's Cathedral and there I encountered the Holy Spirit in such a powerful way.

When the Holy Spirit came upon me, I was paralysed. I mean literally. My legs went soft like jelly. For 20 minutes the fire was rushing through my body and I couldn't move. I felt like every cell in me was going to explode. I said: "Lord enough, I can't take it anymore."

Jesus said when you receive the baptism of the Holy Spirit, you receive *power*.

That was the huge turning point in my life. I had a God encounter. I remember not walking out of the cathedral, I floated out. I experienced joy unspeakable. Peace I couldn't explain.

I said I am going to get serious about God.

I went to university for four years, I was on the Dean's list, I got this great job at DBS. I knew I had a call of God for ministry, but every year, I would say: "Lord, I'm ready for full-time ministry, if you call me I will quit my job now and I will come and serve you." And the Lord said: "You are not ready. I want you to work in the secular world for a while."

"If I can trust the bank to credit my salary, why can't I trust the living God to take care of me?"

So I waited. Then, one year, I got promoted, then I got promoted again. My bosses said: "You know, Yang, if you stay in this company, you have a great future."

And the Holy Spirit said: "Now I want you to quit your job!"

It was the most difficult decision – man, I struggled because I didn't know where the provision was going to come from. Our church was in a very rudimentary phase. I was going to pay myself $800 a month. I didn't know how I was going to survive.

So I said to the Lord: "If You can show me You can provide for me, I'll quit my job and come to full-time ministry." The Lord said: "No, you quit your job, and I'll show you I can provide for you."

Faith is spelt R-I-S-K. When I was working in DBS, every 27th of the month, the bank would credit my salary. If I can trust the bank to credit my salary, why can't I trust the living God to take care of me?

So I took that bungee step of faith into full-time ministry. We sold our home. We moved into a rented facility. We had garage sale after garage sale. We sold everything we could just to get by.

And I tell you this – this is my 30th year in full-time ministry and my path drips with abundance. God has blessed me beyond my wildest imagination and God has blessed the church.

So, I'm going to encourage you to trust the Lord in this journey. If He calls you, then He will pay the bills. He will take care of you.

DO YOU HAVE SOME PRACTICAL ADVICE FOR RUNNING THE RACE WELL?

1. HAVE A ROBUST DEVOTIONAL LIFE

My day starts with prayer and devotion. I want to encourage you to keep your devotional life strong, keep it robust. If you keep the fire burning, I promise you the fire will keep you burning for God.

You have to fan and feed the fire, you have to make sure there is a flow of oil in your life.

I used to take walks every morning, to fellowship with and talk to God.

> At the end of the day, if I finish well, it's because God has shown mercy to me.

One day, the Lord told me: "Don't just do your devotions the moment you get up. Set aside time every day so I can meet with you."

So I decided to wake up every morning at 4:45am to spend time with God.

Amazingly, I am rarely woken by the alarm clock, no matter how tired I am. There are many mornings where I wake up, look at my clock and see that it's 4:44 am. Just one minute before my alarm goes off.

When that happens, I get so happy because God is more interested in meeting me than I sometimes am to meet Him. He says: "Get up, it's time for our fellowship!"

Thirty years in full-time ministry – the longer I know Him, the sweeter He becomes.

2. STAY TRUSTING

Trust His faithfulness, trust His goodness because that's what's going to carry you through the long term.

Romans 9:16 says that it is not him who wills, nor him who runs, but God who shows mercy.

At the end of the day, if I finish well, it's because God has shown mercy to me.

Justice is getting what we deserve, but mercy is receiving what we do not deserve.

> "Our Father has a plan and purpose for our lives – this motivates me to want to finish this race well."

Mercy is a good deal – much like the one the 11th-hour worker received in Jesus' parable of the workers in Matthew 20. He worked only for an hour, but he earned a whole day's wage of one denarius. Like him, we all have gotten what we do not deserve from the Lord, our Master.

But will you continue to be like the first-hour workers, who ended up upset with their wages and complained to the master? Will you haggle with Him and demand what you want, or are you going to trust that God will fight for and defend you?

Without trust in the Lord and His goodness, you will not finish well.

Learn to give thanks to God. Every morning, I find 15 things that I thank God for – the many things that He has done in my life. I want to encourage you to find 10 things you can thank God for every day – if not 10, then five things. But start somewhere.

Being grateful and trusting in Him is a very important part of the journey.

3. STAY CONNECTED

Stay connected with God, and with the people God has placed in your life. This is an important part of our journey; we need one another to finish well on this pilgrimage.

4. STAY UNCLUTTERED

Remember that your happiness is not predicated on what you have on this earth but what God has given to you.

I totally dislike clutter, and my church members even call me the spiritual Marie Kondo because I throw away everything that can be thrown away!

> "In a marathon, the last 100m is the hardest. You just have to keep pressing on with God."

The Christian life is a pilgrimage, by the time you finish the race you want to be totally uncluttered.

After all, this life is a probationary one, a dress room rehearsal, a parenthesis in eternity.

Just live this life simply and finish this race well. Recognising that each and every one of us was conceived in the mind of God even before we were conceived in our mothers' wombs, that our Father has a plan and purpose for our lives – understanding this really motivates me to want to finish this race well.

Since God has a plan for my life, an aspiration that He wants me to achieve, I want to finish this race well, serve this generation and fulfil the will of God.

In a marathon, the last 100m is the hardest. You just have to keep moving on, you just have to keep pressing on with God.

◆ **Text by Anna Cheang**

Leadership

The secret behind the late property maverick Thio Gim Hock's success

"As I go about God's kingdom work, I can see God's hand in every bit of my career. He helps me with my career and He gives me hope for the future," says Mr Thio Gim Hock, CEO of OUE, in an August 2019 talk. Photo by Geraldine Tan.

Mr Thio Gim Hock has an impressive resume. Despite being 81 years old, he continues to helm publicly-listed OUE. He is known for his sharp business acumen and innovative business ideas but above all, the guts to swim against the tide.

When asked what it is that has helped him to excel in his career, he is quick to tell you.

"All the developments were very successful because God's hand was in it. I began to learn how to pray for God's help in whatever I did."

"As I go about God's kingdom work, I can see God's hand in every bit of my career."

"Be faithful. Seek God; seek first His kingdom and His righteousness and I am very sure all these things will be added unto you," Thio told a rapt crowd of about 200 people at a lunchtime talk, referencing Matthew 6:33.

His audience had gathered in the heart of Singapore's central business district (CBD) to hear him speak at a talk entitled, *Grow*, organised by FCBC Marketplace Connect.

"As I go about God's kingdom work, I can see God's hand in every bit of my career. He helps me with my career and He gives me a hope for the future." (Jeremiah 29:11)

Thio would know this well, having steered the real estate companies he was in through the 1997 Asian Financial Crisis and the 2008 Global Financial Crisis. The industry was battered during the crises as business sentiment nosedived and property prices plunged.

NAVIGATING TOUGH TIMES

The 1997 crisis sent Singapore's property market into decline and remained subdued till early 2000s. During this time, Thio was CEO for Target Realty, a subsidiary of City Developments Limited (CDL). The company had quite a few projects gestating; one of them was a big piece of land in the CBD and they did not know what to do with it.

"It was an open planning plot, therefore, you could do anything. They wanted to do office, hotel, all that … it didn't work out."

He committed the matter to the Lord and was reminded of a project he had overseen in London. "So I said, 'Why don't we do 100% residential apartments?'"

Mr Thio's advice to HPL to purchase land at Canary Wharf was God-inspired. The project, Canary Riverside (*left, foreground*), went on to do well. Photo by Joseph Gilbey on Unsplash.

His suggestion was met with incredulity as the project would create some 1,000 apartments in a down market.

"If we do that, it will be the first project where we have apartments in the city. And city living is very popular," he explained.

He had proposed a similar idea while he was an executive director at Hotel Properties Limited (HPL), urging the company to buy a plot of land at Canary Wharf which, at that time, was considered the backwater of London. HPL heeded his advice and the residential project was not only oversubscribed, it also commanded the same high prices as in London's West End.

CDL mulled over the idea but only began construction of the project after Thio left. Today, The Sail, mainly made up of residential apartments, occupies that plot of land.

But that is not all.

WISDOM FROM ABOVE

During his early days as CEO and group managing director of Overseas Union Enterprises (before it took over OUE), he proposed moving Mandarin Hotel's lobby to the fifth floor, and turning the first four floors into retail space.

"It was a great decision that the Lord helped me make," shared Thio as it helped create $550 million in value for the company.

The company also had a multi-storey carpark in its portfolio, which was generating about $1 million in annual revenue.

Mr Thio standing at the lobby of OUE Bayfront, which was previously a multi-storey carpark. He tells how God gave him the idea to turn it into a office building, more than tripling the land's revenue stream. Photo courtesy of Mr Thio Gim Hock.

"But it wasn't a good use of land. We studied it and discovered we had permission to build an office, so it is where our present office is now. And we put that in the real estate investment trust for $1.1 billion, all with the help of God," revealed Thio.

He also attributes God for the bold idea to implement a deferred payment scheme for the Twin Peaks condominium project. Sales stalled following the government's property cooling measures. The scheme helped to turn things around.

"In my work, I always pray, 'God, tell me how to do this.' When we have problems, I always ask Him for help on how to solve the problems.

"God gave the ideas – new ideas, new designs, the way to layout, the pricing. He put those in my mind, they were all from God. They were all successful and the company made a lot of money.

"As you serve God, God gives you these ideas. Sometimes you think it's your own idea but when you reflect back, you know it is Him."

SERVING GOD AT WORK

Thio's life was transformed at 50, when he encountered God for the first time. Up till then, despite seemingly having it all – high-flying career, happy marriage, three loving children – there was an unexplainable emptiness which he later found out was a God-shaped hole in his heart.

He was born into a Christian family and while he identified himself as a believer, he did not have a relationship with God.

That encounter in 1988 ignited a fervour within him to get to know God, read the Bible and share the Good News with everyone he met.

The following year, God put a burden on his heart to start a lunchtime office fellowship in HPL. It started with five people meeting weekly in the boardroom and it soon outgrew the location, as 50 to 60 would gather.

Mr Thio makes it a point to commit all his staff and the projects he is working on to the Lord. Photo from Mandarin Orchard Singapore's Facebook page.

"Many people were saved. We prayed for the sick and many people were healed. And because they were healed, they begin to believe and they brought their families in," recalled Thio.

It was not just his staff that he reached out to.

"Salespeople will come and try to set up a meeting and normally, you send it to your staff. But I would say, 'Okay, come to my office to promote your product. But on one condition – after you finish, you give me equal time, you listen to me,'" he said.

"I'll share the Gospel with them and I led many of them, on their knees in my office, to the Lord. I took advantage of my position," confessed Thio, drawing laughter from the office crowd.

"Once you know Christ, you can't help but talk about Him!"

◆Text by Geraldine Tan

Editor's Note: The late Mr Thio Gim Hock went home to the Lord in April 2020.

Leadership

"If you just give money, how do you change a person's heart?": Why Fullerton Markets CEO Mario Singh is hands-on at his foundation

Mario and Shalyn Singh set up Soulrich Foundation to start giving their wealth away early. All photos courtesy of Mario Singh.

On the day that the article of him setting up a charity made the headlines in *The Straits Times*, the first question that Mario Singh's two young children excitedly asked him was: "Daddy, you're a millionaire?"

To the 44-year-old entrepreneur, that's an irrelevant question. It is not about how much you have or do not have; it is what you do with it that matters.

The CEO and founder of brokerage firm Fullerton Markets is giving his wealth away through Soulrich Foundation, established with his wife and mother last year. They plan to give away $80,000 this year, with the amount raised to $100,000 next year. As of May 2020, they've already disbursed $35,000.

Mario Singh wanted to give in a way that is proactive, scalable and sustainable.

While Elliot and Chantelle, eight and ten years old respectively, are probably still too young to question why their parents are giving away their inheritance, Singh has been trying to instil in them the importance of helping others through their regular delivery of food to the needy.

He also tells the children what investor Warren Buffett famously said: "I'll give my children enough money so that they would feel they could do anything but not so much that they could do nothing."

"If the Lord wills it and we sell the business for $100 million, the bulk of it is obviously going to go to Soulrich Foundation and not to their pockets. So they'd better be prepared for that," Singh added with a hearty laugh.

A FOUNDATION THAT OUTLIVES THEM

Not satisfied with ad hoc donations to charity, which he calls "reactive giving", Singh wanted to give in a way that is proactive, scalable and sustainable. "Reactive giving is like if I have excess, I'll help you," he explained. "It's time to take that step of faith to be more proactive in our initiatives."

He is also keenly aware that, by himself, his funds are limited. He is hoping to tap into his circle of high net worth friends to add to the kitty by another 50%.

"Our lives are limited but the foundation shouldn't be," he added. "I want it to outlive and outgrow us, to carry on the good work."

This was why Singh went about setting up a charity that is a grantmaker with the status of an Institution of a Public Character (IPC). Little did he know that it would end up being an arduous process of eight months.

Soulrich Foundation was finally registered in March 2020.

"I want it to outlive and outgrow us, to carry on the good work."

While the foundation is not allowed to raise funds publicly, private donations are eligible for the 250% tax reduction.

The charity currently supports 11 beneficiaries under three pillars: Well-being (Food from the Heart, The New Charis Mission), family (Focus on the Family, Centre for Fathering) and Christian education (The Bible Society of Singapore, Alpha).

Citing Proverbs 3:27, which says: "Do not withhold good from those to whom it is due, when it is in your power to do it" as his guiding principle for the foundation, Singh let on that he initially wanted to have as many as 10 pillars but his homemaker wife, Shalyn, 52, reined him in so they could focus.

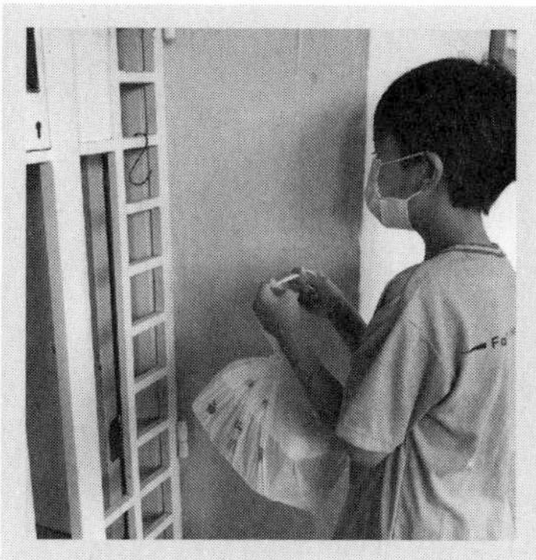

Elliot, 8, has been going with his parents to deliver food to the needy. Singh believes in getting his children involved so that they understand the importance of helping others.

The Singh family regularly volunteers at soup kitchen Willing Hearts, also a beneficiary of the foundation. Singh said that the amount of food given out during the COVID-19 period has gone up from 6,000 packets a day to 8,300.

Shalyn (*right*) hands over some bread to an old folks' home during one of the family's bread runs.

DO WHAT JESUS DID

Going beyond just giving money, Singh and his family help soup kitchen Willing Hearts deliver 450 packets of food every Monday and Thursday.

On other days they collect bread from bakeries and restaurants and drop them off at old folks' homes. He and Shalyn were also about to start being mentors to disadvantaged teenagers when COVID-19 put the brakes on all activities.

It was through one of the food delivery trips that he got to know a 98-year-old man living on his own, with a helper for assistance, in a one-room flat. Singh has since gone back to visit a few times, chatting, eating and building up a relationship with him.

"It doesn't really take your heart to give money because it comes out of your abundance," said Singh. "But when you get involved, it really shows you the Lord's heart. If you just give money, how do you change a person's heart, how do you lead them to Jesus?"

FROM CLEANER TO TRADER

The middle child of an Indian father and Chinese mother – and named after the writer of his father's favourite *The Godfather* series – Singh grew up going to church with his mother and two siblings.

At 16, his father died from a heart attack at home on Christmas eve. Overnight, his mother, a primary school teacher, became the family's sole breadwinner and struggled to raise the children.

"If you just give money, how do you change a person's heart, how do you lead them to Jesus?"

Singh ended up studying chemical engineering in the National University of Singapore. "I studied like crazy but came out with third-class honours. It shattered my mum's dreams," he recalled.

He could not find a job. After a three-month stint with a local company that built bio-hazard cabinets, Singh in his late twenties set up a cleaning company that did the housework for young families who did not want a live-in helper.

It was then that a few of his close friends started dabbling in currency trading and Singh thought to himself: "If I want to make big money, I must be in the money business."

Mario Singh was the only one from Asia and, in his words, "the smallest mosquito" to attend a retreat for "kingdom traders" held by renowned author Peter Wagner at his ranch in Colorado.

AGAINST ALL RATIONALITY

At 32, after a few years of forex trading, Singh started FX1, an academy to teach financial education. "It just boomed probably because it was one of the first of its kind," he recounted.

A major turning point came when he was invited to go on business news channel CNBC to give his market views. His credibility was further boosted when he subsequently appeared on international media more than 40 times.

But three years later, by 2011, the academy was failing. Singh fell out with his business partners and was close to shutting down the business.

> "It went against all rationality but the Lord laid it upon my heart that we have to keep the business."

It was also at this time that renowned author Peter Wagner, after a visit to Singh's church then, invited him to attend a four-day retreat for "kingdom traders" at his house in Colorado, US. (The last book that Wagner wrote was *The Great Transfer of Wealth: Financial Release for Advancing God's Kingdom*.)

"It's not a problem in getting more money, it's a problem when money gets to you," said Singh, calling the salvation of his soul his greatest treasure.

"We were down to our last few thousand dollars and Shalyn was pregnant with Elliot then. It was an honest step of faith and I went," said Singh. "I was the only one from Asia and I was the smallest mosquito there."

He returned to Singapore inspired to be a good steward of money, with a renewed conviction that he should keep the business.

"My wife wanted me to shut it, I wanted to pour in our remaining funds. It was one of the biggest fights we ever had," Singh mused. "It went against all rationality but the Lord laid it upon my heart that we have to keep it, so I did. And we turned it around."

MAKING MONEY

Today the academy has become the training arm of Fullerton Markets, which Singh founded in 2016 and has about 120 employees here and in the region.

The brokerage firm remains his main source of income, but he also gets revenue from speaking engagements as well as businesses he owns in marketing and events, as well as fintech and IT solutions.

No stranger to Christians who view trading as gambling, Singh makes it very clear that they are totally different.

> "Money doesn't change who you are; it magnifies who you are."

"Gambling is punting, where you don't know when to get out and you end up getting into huge debts. That's what casinos are," he explained. "At its most basic, trading or investing is about buying low and selling high. Even when asset prices are dropping, you can sell first and buy later, and still make a profit in between. That's the financial market."

To Singh, the parable of the talents in Matthew 25 *is* about making money – it's about what you do with money and how you generate a good yield, he added.

"Money doesn't change who you are; it magnifies who you are. If you've been giving small amounts, when you get more, you'll give more," said Singh.

"I know that I want to increase the giving to Soulrich Foundation every year. We have resolved upfront that money doesn't play a big part in our lives. We're not soul-tied to money."

◆Text by Jane Lee

Leadership

"God directed me from the beginning": Singaporean Lawrence Tong on leading Operation Mobilisation worldwide

Despite the disruptions to OM ministries all over the world, international director Lawrence Tong is trusting that God is in control. Photo courtesy of OM International.

He is a Singaporean who leads one of the largest mission agencies in the world. And Lawrence Tong, International Director of Operation Mobilisation (OM), leads with three tenets: Agitate. Innovate. Orchestrate.

Tong's visionary leadership and constant reach for excellence are well known. But what stands out most are not the leadership qualities you might expect.

DREAMERS, VISIONARIES AND PIONEERS

When Tong took the reins in 2013, the first task he set himself was to change the mission statement.

"The mission statement used to be a paragraph long!" Tong exclaimed. "On the websites of all 46 OM fields, each one had its own statement. None of them aligned.

"So I said, no good, we've got to do something."

> "What gets me excited every day is the thought that 4,000 OM-ers can mobilise a million people into the mission field!"

That *something* was 172 two-hour, face-to-face interviews with OM leaders across the globe and an internal survey where they collected 1,400 detailed responses in more than eight languages.

Undaunted, Tong wanted to hear directly from OM-ers: "They are the people giving their life to this movement; I want to know their concerns, their frustrations and aspirations."

It took 18 months, busting the widely-touted "100-day grace period" that leaders are said to have for initiating change.

What emerged was a 13-word purpose statement that embodied OM-ers' values. It was quickly and unanimously adopted.

OM itself is not unfamiliar with change.

In fact, it is an organisation founded by dreamers, visionaries and pioneers who started by smuggling Bibles into Eastern Europe, then buying a ship – and eventually three more over the next 40 years – that went around the world bringing knowledge, help and hope.

THE FLOATING BOOKSHOP

Tong's history with OM started in 1974 when the young Christian

The MV Logos, the very first ship owned by OM Ships International

During her service, the MV Doulos held the world record for the oldest ocean-going passenger ship – she was built in 1914, just two years after the Titanic.

stepped onboard the *MV Logos*, the very first ship owned by OM Ships International.

Docked in Singapore at the old World Trade Centre, the *Logos* was in a constant flurry of activity. Crew members from around the world were hard at work – some were running the book exhibition onboard, others were busy with regular maintenance duties and still others were engaging Singaporean visitors.

Many were young men and women who had left their homes and set aside two years of their lives to serve onboard the floating bookshop.

"What attracted me to the ship? I saw these people whose lives were totally sold for the Lord Jesus Christ," Tong recalled. To the 17-year-old who had only accepted Christ a year ago, that passion was contagious.

After National Service in 1978, Tong signed up for a two-year commitment to serve on the *MV Doulos*, OM's second ship with a crew of 350 people from over 50 countries.

Tong was a hard-worker – from young, he had helped out in his father's small stationery business with his siblings.

But he confesses to having rough edges. "I have a pretty strong personality. I speak my mind."

He says of his younger self: "When I saw something that was not right, I *always* offered my unsolicited opinion. People didn't really like it."

> The Lord spoke to him:
> "As long as you are in Christian service, never again ask for any promotion or assignment."

After applying to – and receiving rejections from – the leaders of two of the most easy-going departments onboard, Tong was devastated.

"The chief steward told me that he didn't want me in his department!" And the other advised him that he was not ready for the field – Tong was the only applicant in the entire intake who was rejected.

Tong was eventually assigned to the book exhibition department.

It prompted a deep search. One afternoon, Tong was praying as he worked in the solitary confines of the bookhold, located far below deck near the hull.

There, he sensed the Lord speaking to him: "As long as you are in Christian service, never again ask for any promotion or assignment.

"That has been my guiding principle until this day," said Tong.

Tong (*right*) with his teammate in a temporary line-up office. Line-up teams are advance parties of three or four members sent ahead to various ports-of-call to prepare for the ship's arrival. At each port-of-call, teams need to work with everyone from governments, to NGOs, businessmen and even welfare organisations to arrange official permits, organise ministry opportunities, raise funds for sponsorship and execute publicity campaigns. When the ship arrives, the team moves back onboard and runs all the programmes that have been organised for the ship's visit.

GOD OF THE IMPOSSIBLE

Soon, Tong was invited to work in the programme office where he discovered his organisational skills. He was subsequently asked to join the line-up team.

At 23, Tong was tasked to lead his first line-up team to Puerto Cabello, a small port of about 100,000 people and only 13 churches. His instructions were clear: Prepare a short programme for the *Doulos* visit.

He had six weeks to do so, but by the end of the second, Tong had spoken to and visited all 13 churches and their pastors. With a month left, Tong decided to extend his preparations to Valencia, a city of about a million people that was an hour's drive away.

Communications in the 1970s were still through telex messages which took days, so Tong made a judgement call: He sent an update to the leaders and left.

Lawrence Tong by the quayside when the Doulos arrived at Puerto Cabello, Venezuela.

"I couldn't wait for their blessings, so I just went ahead because I felt that it was within my purview as team leader to step up and do something."

When the ship's leaders were told of Tong's decisions, they were not pleased – but it was too late, Tong was already in Valencia, actively promoting the ship.

It turned out to be one of the *Doulos*' most successful visits to Latin America.

Tong eventually spent 10 years doing line-up with the *Doulos*, which he describes as "the best hands-on leadership development anyone could ask for – in terms of exposure, skills and total dependence on God for the impossible".

In 1990, a year after Tong married Susan, whom he had met on the ship, the pair left OM. Tong wanted to start a business.

"I thought that running a small business would give me the flexibility of time to serve in whatever capacity the Lord led me," he said.

> "I remembered that formational experience in the bookhold where I would go wherever my leaders asked me to."

It did – during his 10 years in business, Tong helped OM Ships start their fund-raising efforts in Asia and served on the board of OM Singapore.

In 2000, Tong and Susan rejoined OM full-time when Tong was invited to lead the *MV Logos II* as the first Asian ship director.

Tong said: "It seems to me that God somehow kept me with a foothold in OM, so that I was never really out of the picture."

He was not just in the picture, but placed in roles with increasing responsibilities.

Lawrence Tong (*second from right*) with OM Singapore colleagues including Rodney Hui (*far left*) who was OM Singapore's first national director.

While onboard the *Logos II*, Tong received another assignment: OM wanted to start a work in China and the leaders were convinced that he was the right person for it; would he take it on?

Tong was disappointed. "It felt like they wanted me elsewhere. I told Susan, 'I think I just got fired.'"

But again, as Tong prayed about it, he knew it was where the Lord wanted him to be. "I remembered that formational experience in the bookhold where I would go wherever my leaders asked me to."

And so he went to China.

LORD, LET ME LEAD

There was one assignment, however, that took Tong a much longer time to accept.

OM International was looking for its next International Director in 2012 and the search committee wanted Tong to throw his name in the hat. He declined, but six months later, they called again.

The chairman of the committee asked him to at least talk to them. "I said okay, but I never took them seriously," Tong laughed.

During the interview, as Tong was pressed on why he would not consider the job, he shared that all the questions he was being asked were management questions, and he didn't want to *manage* OM.

So what do you want, they asked. "Let me lead. Ask me leadership questions – my dreams and what change I want to see," Tong challenged.

"To their credit, they did. And I began to respond, interact and debate … I told them everything!

"I thought, let them decide what they think about it. After all, there's no risk to me, I'm not going to be the international director, this is just my contribution."

Little did he know that, at the end of the search process, he was the only candidate left. Lawrence Tong took over the role of International Director in 2013 and was re-elected for a second term in 2017.

(*From left*) Peter Maiden, George Verwer, the founder of OM, with his iconic world map jacket, and Lawrence Tong at OM's 60th Anniversary celebrations in 2017.

> "A key question that drives him to reject the status quo is: Is this all we can do?"

Under Tong's watch, OM's mission statement was not the only thing that was overhauled.

Tong inherited a team of 22 seasoned OM leaders in the global leadership team. They were great people, godly and faithful, but Tong was not satisfied.

"This will not take us into the future," Tong said, referring to the logistical and practical problems of the leadership structure. So he came up with a proposal for a revamp – one that called for a drastic change of the global leadership team.

Lawrence Tong with six of OM's Associate Directors who form the Global Leadership team.

The OM International board of directors was eventually established in September 2017. Among other things, it provides governance oversight of all OM ministries.

"Amongst the 22 leaders, I was the third youngest. Today, I'm the oldest amongst eight highly-motivated, fast-paced Generation X-ers," declared the 62-year-old Tong. "I must prepare a new generation of leaders to take over."

When the previous leaders resigned, they gave him their blessings: "Do what you need to do to take this organisation forward for God."

"That really humbled me," Tong recounted. "It was a reflection of God's goodness to me."

Another key change that Tong instituted was to install an international board of directors above himself.

He recognised that, in current conditions of charity law and strict governance, the lack of a board was unhealthy for any organisation. Oversight and accountability needed to be established.

Now, Tong says: "I lead from the middle, not from the top."

A MILLION FOR THE MISSION FIELD

"I don't get excited growing OM. What gets me excited every day is the thought that 4,000 OM-ers can mobilise a million people into the mission field!" said Tong.

"That is the beauty of the life of every Christian: All the experiences you've had in the past? God can call them into His service."

A key question that drives him to reject the status quo is: "Is this all we can do?"

He declared: "I believe in a God who is not bound by human limitations. And I also believe in a God who wants us to do better."

From volunteering "unsolicited opinions" to being sought out for each leadership role that holds a greater responsibility than the last, Lawrence Tong is a leader moulded from the inside out.

Today, one life that has been changed by God is now spearheading change in and through one of the largest missions organisations in the world.

"God has directed me from the very beginning, I'm just a small chess piece," Tong noted. "That is the beauty of the life of every Christian: All the experiences you've had in the past? God can call them into His service.

◆ **Text by Tan Huey Ying**

He sold his companies, donated his assets and became a janitor: YMCA CEO Steve Loh's headlong journey into missions

"How do I preach the Gospel in strategic business decisions? How do I be a servant leader of hundreds?" YMCA CEO Steve Loh asks himself every day. Photo courtesy of YMCA Singapore.

Who would voluntarily go from heading three companies to becoming an unpaid janitor?

That would be Steve Loh.

Loh had an illustrious career in the media industry, complete with three companies under his name, when he gave it all up to become an unpaid janitor at missions organisation Youth With a Mission (YWAM Singapore).

It was not a decision that came easily. Nor was it one that he lived with effortlessly.

For two whole years after he surrendered everything to God, he would weep during worship, mourning his losses and fearing for his future.

"Man, in the Creator's view and intent, was not made to be selfish ... when we are, something within us dies."

Yet, with this painful sacrifice came a greater reward – an immense joy and freedom that flowed from living out a higher purpose his Heavenly Father had carved out for him. One that was much more fulfilling than self-centred pursuits, said Loh, now 47.

"Man, in the Creator's view and intent, was not made to be selfish. And when we are – and I am, there's no two ways about it – something within us dies," he said.

Looking back on the past 13 years of his service in YWAM Singapore and YMCA, where he is now chief executive officer and general secretary, he added: "Missions was God's redeeming grace to save me from myself, to save me from an empty life."

DIVINE DISCONTENTMENT

Back in the early 2000s, while in the prime of his career, Loh felt a deep emptiness that did not seem to make sense.

After all, he was running three lucrative businesses – a production house, a digital rental company and a Wagyu beef distribution. He had a dazzling resumé that included being a radio and news presenter at big names like local broadcaster Mediacorp and sports channel ESPN.

He was earning enough to be debt-free by the time he was 34 and could easily afford the trappings of modern society, including a private condominium and a car.

"The more I was focused on a very comfortable retirement, the emptier I felt."

Yet, despite this and the fact that he was actively attending and serving in church, he felt a hollowness he now describes as a "deep divine discontentment".

"Even though I was enjoying the blessings of Singapore life, which I recognise are from God, life ironically became quite empty. It almost felt like the more I tried to fill it, the emptier it got," he said.

"The verse in Matthew 16:25, which says, 'For whoever would save his life will lose it, but whoever loses his life for my sake will find it' really rung true for me. The more I was focused on that fulfilment of self, trying to save my life – literally by saving my money, my career, my man-made plans, my 25-year trajectory for myself and a very comfortable retirement – the emptier I felt."

COSTLY DISCIPLESHIP

And so began his search for purpose.

During this time, in 2007, one of his business partners and close friends left the company to join YWAM Singapore's Discipleship Training School (DTS), a six-month programme that seeks to nurture and train Christians in their God-given identity through lectures and hands-on missions experience.

After the first week, his friend rang him up.

"He said, 'Steve, these YWAMers are amazing. They hear God's voice, they all live together and they all work for free. And there are 25,000 of them worldwide!'

"I was like, oh no, you've joined a cult! I'm coming to visit you immediately," Loh recalled with a laugh.

"Where in the Bible does it say that discipleship is safe?"

He dropped in for a day, planning to check out what exactly his friend had gotten himself into. Unexpectedly, however, he was so gripped by what he was seeing that he asked to stay for another week, and another, and another, and eventually completed the entire six months.

Apart from the sessions of deep worship and learning, it was the faith of those he met in YWAM Singapore that made him experience God in a way he never had before.

"I was surrounded by people of faith who truly believed the Bible and had given up everything for God to live out the Great Commission. When you're surrounded by such people, you, too, encounter God.

"It was like what Job said in Job 42:5. 'My ears had heard of you but now my eyes have seen you'," he said.

Even though Loh had grown up in a loving Christian family where authentic faith and grace were lived out daily, he still had to make his own decision to courageously answer the call to discipleship.

He attributes his decision to go into missions to the relentless prayers of his parents for him, as well as the way they represented the love of the Lord in always accepting, providing and championing him.

"One can never overstate the role parents play in their child's discipleship into the ways of Christ.

"My personal theology back then was that if I follow God, He will bless me financially and nothing too bad will happen to me. One of the reasons why I followed God so closely was for those reasons, to keep my risks low, to make my life as easy as possible."

"Their risks were high, their life was hard and their joy was full."

But when he began to study Scripture more intently, he realised that he had been dead wrong.

"Look at the life of the disciples. When they put up their hand to follow Jesus, their lives were anything but safe. Peter was martyred,

Apostle Paul was jailed, beaten and shipwrecked three times, Stephen was stoned to death, and the list goes on. Where in the Bible does it say that discipleship is safe?"

Despite the risks involved in true discipleship, he saw how sold out for God those at YWAM Singapore were: "In John Piper's words, their risks were high, their life was hard and their joy was full."

This deeply challenged his faith.

WHO IS JESUS TO YOU?

Loh was further confronted with his own beliefs during a week called Lordship Week, where he found himself examining his heart more closely.

"I loved the Lord but not enough.
It was too much to give up."

The questions were direct: Who is Jesus Christ to you? Is He not just your Saviour but also your Lord? Is He your Boss, your King, your Master?

Loh remembers clearly it was on a Tuesday that they read the story of the rich young ruler in Mark 10:17-22 who asked Jesus what he must do to inherit eternal life.

Like the rich young ruler, he had lived his life faithfully following the commandments of Christ. But there is one thing you lack, he heard the Holy Spirit say to him, just as Jesus had told the man: Sell everything, give to the poor and follow Me (Mark 10:21).

Loh's answer was swift: No.

"I realised that I can read the Bible my
whole life yet not believe it."

"Are you kidding?" he asked God. "I've spent the last 14 years building up my career, my resumé, my talents, my clientele, my

Steve with his wife, Priscilla, and their children, Faith, 12, and David, 9. Photo courtesy of Steve Loh.

three companies. Give everything up and come follow You?

"I actually told God, no. I was in tears, just like the rich young ruler was, because I loved the Lord but not enough. It was too much to give up.

"To me, finances equaled security. In my business days, what would give me peace that surpasses all understanding was my bank account balance. I would come home and check it every night. Financial security had become the idol of my life."

He went home and processed this encounter with his wife, who strongly encouraged him to obey. Nevertheless, he continued to struggle with the Lord.

But three days later, his resistance turned into surrender after the Lord convicted his heart.

"I realised that I can read the Bible my whole life yet not believe it. I can read about how God is good my whole life, yet never walk in that knowledge or trust Him. If God is as good as the Bible says, then why am I not giving up everything to follow Him?

"Because I'm not sure. I wonder: What if He doesn't deliver me? What if He doesn't come through for me? What if Matthew 6:33 is not true?

"I was thinking it's better have one foot in, one foot out. Some faith in God and some faith in myself. It's safer to be lukewarm. But the Lord said to me, either you're hot or you're cold. If you're lukewarm, I'll spit you out (Revelation 3:15-16)."

FROM BUSINESS OWNER TO JANITOR

Thus, with much fear and trembling, Loh obeyed.

By the end of that same year, he closed down all his companies, donated all his assets to YWAM Singapore and joined the organisation, beginning his missions journey humbly – as a janitor.

"There was a need and I put my hand up," he said simply. "I felt I needed the humility." The role was also unpaid, as are all roles in YWAM, as staff have to raise their own income.

"I made sure that I had the cleanest toilet ... The pleasure and presence of God over me was my great reward."

For a whole year, he spent his time doing all sorts of tasks required to keep the place running, from cleaning toilets and mopping floors to painting walls and constructing beds.

"I loved it, coming from a very, very stressful corporate life to just making sure that I had the cleanest toilet that YWAM has ever seen," he said. "The pleasure and presence of God over me was my great reward."

That humbling year also taught him that he is not defined by what he does, Loh said.

"What defines me is what my identity is in Christ as the child of the Most High, and that set me up for the next decade of missions work. I had a lot of security in whatever God called me to do. I didn't have to worry about rank, title or politics."

The Lord also proved to him and his family that He would take care of them financially, no matter the circumstance: "God provided always. Every year, every month. There were some scary months, but He always provides when the time is right and when it's in His plans."

CREATED TO WORSHIP

The following year, he became the school leader of DTS and subsequently was appointed its director a few years later.

"We were created to fully serve a living God ... until we do that, we never really find out who we are."

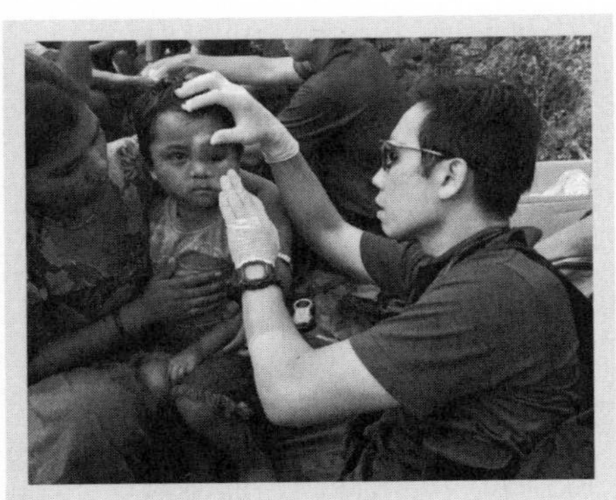

His time at YWAM Singapore saw Steve participate in rescue relief work, such as during the 2015 Nepal Earthquake. "It was God's grace over me that I became so captured by the needs of others that I found very little capacity, very little time, to worry about myself," he said.

In total, he spent 12 years in YWAM Singapore and counts this decision the best one he has ever made.

"My great reward was meeting God in my field of obedience," he said. "I discovered joy in living out my intended purpose, which is to do the good works that God has prepared in advance for me to do in Christ (Ephesians 2:10).

"In reaching out and preaching the Gospel, I got to discover that we were always created to worship. We were always created to fully serve a living God. Not partially, but fully. And until we do that, we never really find out who we are.

"All of us were created for a purpose which has an eternal impact, but most of us never walk in it. We are that aeroplane that sits on the tarmac and never flies. We are that ship that sits on the highway. We never fulfil our destiny.

"But being in missions allowed me to discover who I was in Christ and to live that out fearfully. It was a place of great joy for me. It still is."

CALLED TO GO

He added that fulfilling God's purposes for us does not necessarily mean moving to a different country to become missionaries in the traditional sense of the word.

"All of us were created for a purpose which has an eternal impact, but most of us never walk in it."

"Being a missionary is a state of the heart. I have met hundreds of missionaries who are CEOs of multinational corporations, lawyers, doctors, captains of industries, small business owners, taxi drivers, cafe owners, all very much with what appears to be regular jobs.

"But they've made Jesus Lord, they've made a promise to fulfil the Great Commission and to represent the character of Christ, and they're doing it in their sphere of influence."

In fact, this has been Loh's latest challenge since he left YWAM Singapore in 2018 to head YMCA, whose mandate is not to preach but to serve the community, he said.

"How do I preach the Gospel in strategic business decisions? How do I be a servant leader of hundreds?"

"Traditional missions was easier because it's very straightforward – serve the poor and needy, and preach the Gospel.

"In my current season, however, how do I be a CEO of a charity that runs social enterprises and preach the Gospel in my strategic business decisions? How do I be a servant leader when I have to command hundreds? That's much more difficult."

"Missions was God's redeeming grace to save me from myself, to save me from an empty life," said Steve, now CEO and general secretary of YMCA. Photo courtesy of YMCA.

In any case, the Bible is clear that all of us are called to fulfil the Great Commission (Matthew 28: 19-20) and be lovers and doers of justice and mercy (Micah 6:8), he said.

"Nobody has to wait for a call to missions. Everybody is called to go. The question is where?"

◆ **Text by Gracia Lee**

"God told my pastor, 'Tell Felicia that I am her Father'": Mediacorp actress Felicia Chin, who lost her father to cancer at 17

After encountering God five years ago, Felicia put her trust in Jesus and counts it the best decision she has ever made. She is also an ambassador for World Vision Singapore, and is pictured here with the beneficiaries of the charity during a trip to Myanmar. Photo courtesy of World Vision Singapore.

The first time I went down on my knees to pray to God was in a toilet cubicle. It was in mid-2015. At that time I was facing difficulties at work and my mind was constantly filled with worries and anxieties that just would not go away.

After she prayed to God about her anxieties, Chin felt a "crystal clear clarity", she said. Photo from Felicia Chin's official Facebook page.

Chin was named as one of the Seven Princesses of Mediacorp in 2006 and has been named one of the Top 10 Most Popular Female Artistes in the Star Awards nine times. Photo courtesy of Mediacorp, The Celebrity Agency.

I'm a bit of a thinker, so various questions would pop up in my mind as I worked, distracting me from what I was doing.

This went on for three weeks. My friends tried to help me but nothing worked. The anxiety still overwhelmed me every day. I did not know who to turn to or what to do.

CRYSTAL CLEAR

One day in my desperation, I remembered this God that I had heard about earlier in the year while filming a travelogue in Australia with my softball coach.

During the long road trips, my colleagues and coach would pray to God and sing worship songs to Him in the car together.

It was different from the first time I had heard about God. Even though I didn't know who He was then, I enjoyed this time and felt a sense of peace.

> "God, if You are real, please help me with these worries and anxieties."

This was the God that I thought about as I was in the bathroom one morning, dreading the day ahead as I prepared to take on yet another day of filming and anxiety.

It was quiet and nobody else was there, so in my desperation I knelt down in the cubicle, closed my eyes and said: "God, if You are real, please help me with these worries and anxieties."

Then I left for work.

Almost immediately, all the questions that filled my mind just disappeared. I felt so much clarity – like high definition, crystal clear clarity. I could even ask myself: "Where are the questions?"

It was quite amazing. I thought to myself: "Wow. Who is this God?"

PERFECT LOVE

The next day – I remember it was a Wednesday afternoon – I asked my coach to bring me to church. It wasn't a traditional-looking church, just a rented compound.

When I walked in there were some youths playing basketball, some studying. Just mundane things.

That was the first day that I knew God is love ... I wish someone had told me that earlier.

But once I set foot in the place I felt all my fears disappear. There was an overwhelming sense of love, like waves of love were just crashing on me.

After telling the pastor how I felt, she told me that what I was experiencing is quite biblical, as the Bible says that perfect love expels all fears (1 John 4:18).

I realised that what I was feeling was God's perfect love.

That was the first day that I knew God is love. That was very powerful. It had never occurred to me before. I wish someone had told me that earlier.

LEAP OF FAITH

As I wondered more about God, I began to pray for things that I thought were impossible, asking God to prove Himself real to me.

For example, I vividly remember asking God to let fellow actor Li Nanxing come and share his faith testimony with me. This was not in arrogance. I was just thinking up a scenario that I thought would not be possible as he wasn't filming at that time and there was no way we would bump into each other.

God was hearing my prayers and answering them in ways I could not have imagined.

A few days later another fellow actor, Rayson Tan, whom I was filming with, shared that his faith testimony had been posted on YouTube. I went home to watch it and happened to find Nanxing *da ge*'s testimony there too.

As I was watching the video, it dawned upon me that he was actually sharing his testimony with me! That was my answered prayer! A few months later I also got a signed copy of his book, *The Real Picture*, which details his life story and faith journey.

Through other similar incidents, I began to realise how real God is. I knew that God was hearing my prayers and answering them in ways I could not have imagined.

So when Rayson Tan invited me to attend a church service a few weeks later, I agreed.

The night before the service, I prayed: "God, I know that You are real. If this is for me, can you give me a dream?"

That night I really had a dream where I saw myself walking away from my past, my old self, just away from it all. And then I woke up.

Since 2003, Chin has starred in almost 40 local dramas, including 法网天后, or Legal Eagles. Photo from Felicia Chin's official Facebook page.

During the service's altar call, this dream came into my mind. Even though I was a little apprehensive at first, I took this leap of faith and gave my life to Jesus.

A FATHER'S LOVE

It's been about five years since I made that decision. I see more clearly now that we all need God's love. We all have hurts and need healing in our lives.

I can speak for myself as I have been through pain. I have also experienced His love and healing.

I lost my dad to cancer when I was 17. Since then I always craved a father figure who could guide me in my life and in my search for purpose.

I have been through pain. I have also experienced His love and healing.

I've always tried to live my life in the best way that I could. But there was only so much that I could do because there was only so much that I knew.

I always felt alone, like I had to fend for myself. There were times that I felt so broken, so sad and so lost, but had no one to turn to. I didn't want to speak to my mother about it as I didn't want her to worry for me.

When I was in my 20s, there were two nights that I went to the kitchen at midnight after my mother had slept, knelt on the floor and cried out into the night sky.

The sorrow and loneliness I felt were very powerful emotions. As I sobbed, I remember feeling an ache and a desperation just for a father.

After I received Christ, my pastor did a follow-up session with me. She shared with me that the Lord had told her to start the session at the third lesson: A relationship with the Father.

God had said to her: "Tell Felicia that I am her Father."

Her words brought me right back to those two times more than five years ago where I was alone on the kitchen floor, crying out for a father.

God had said to my pastor:
"Tell Felicia that I am her Father."

God had heard me. He had always been there for me.

I immediately burst into tears and wept. He was always listening, even when I didn't know Him. Even though I was not perfect, even though I was in darkness, He was always so close.

I was never alone and I have an eternal Father in Him. I will always have a Father with me who loves me and who will guide me in my life.

Recently I asked God to let me feel what a Father's love feels like. As I was quiet before Him, I saw a vision of me resting in His lap, in His embrace.

I just want to encourage people who have lost their fathers when they were young. You may not have felt a father's love. But, not to worry, Father God knows what we are going through.

His love is for all of us, no matter our background. He knows and His love is there to heal us, as long as we cry out to Him.

Chin speaks openly about her faith on social media and posts Bible verses on her Instagram account from time to time. Screenshot of Felicia Chin's Instagram account (@ iamfeliciachin).

Sometimes we feel that we don't know where to go or what to do; sometimes we feel like we need to fend for ourselves, sometimes we feel alone and misunderstood. But He is there for us and He understands us 100%.

Though we are broken pieces, He lovingly picks up each piece and makes them into a beautiful vase. A vase that is valued. He wants to heal us and make us whole again.

Doesn't this make you want to know Him?

ABIDING IN HIM

One of the verses I've been meditating on this year is John 15:5, which says: "I am the vine; you are the branches. If you remain in me and I in you, you will bear much fruit; apart from me you can do nothing."

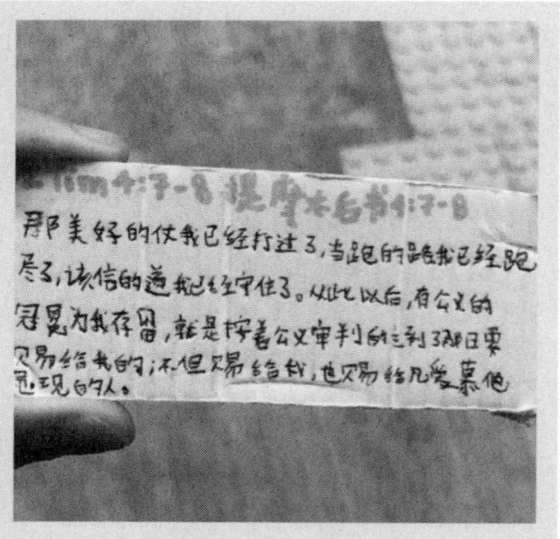

To keep herself pondering on God's Word, Chin writes down verses on used pieces of cardboard and takes it with her wherever she goes. This one here is taken from 2 Timothy 4:7-8. Photo courtesy of Felicia Chin.

I like to write verses on used pieces of cardboard and bring them around with me, pondering them whenever I have empty pockets of time.

I wondered: "What does it mean to abide in Him? Why did Jesus use the analogy of vines and branches?"

As I thought about this verse, I found that the image of vines and branches reminds me of fingers attached to a human body. So Jesus is the body and we are like the fingers.

"Please don't go away. You were made to be with me. Let's do this together."

When Jesus says "apart from me, you can do nothing", He's not saying it in a domineering or oppressive way.

He's saying it out of His love for us. He knows us and made us. He made us to remain in Him because that's the only way that we can have life, we can have joy, we can feel His heartbeat and receive His love and healing.

Can you imagine us detaching ourselves from the body? Of course the individual fingers cannot do anything and will die. It has no life (John 15:6).

But in our defiance we think, no, I want my way. Being with the body is not the best for me. I refuse to remain with the body.

There's a lot of joy and freedom in having His Word and presence in you.

God wants to love us. But if we choose to run away and disconnect ourselves from the body, then how is He supposed to? We are all given a choice.

From this verse, I feel like He is telling me out of His lovingkindness: "Please don't go away. You were made to be with me. Let's do this together." (John 15:9)

An ambassador for World Vision Singapore, she said: "I want to be a vessel of love for Him." She is pictured here with her sponsored children from Myanmar, Kyine Kyine, in a trip last January. Photo courtesy of World Vision Singapore.

What's most important is to be connected to Him first. Then we can draw strength from His love, know His heartbeat and carry out the good works that He has given to us (Ephesians 2:10).

Now whenever I look at my fingers, I'm constantly reminded of this truth. There's a lot of joy and freedom in having His Word and presence in me.

NO ONE LIKE HIM

Sometimes I still feel like I have to be perfect for Him to love me. So, instead of running to Him, I run away from Him when I meet with problems.

But I know that because Jesus died on the cross for my sins, I no longer need to be perfect to be deemed worthy in God's eyes. I can experience this beautiful, deep process of knowing God.

Even in times when I mess up and am angry with myself, He's still there for me and is so patient.

I take comfort in knowing that God is my refuge and my strength (Psalm 46:1). Even when I do not feel it, I set my emotions aside and cling on to this truth. And as I worship Him, I feel His peace, His joy and His love.

Following Jesus is the best decision I've made in my life.

He's the only person in the whole wide world that knows me even more than I know myself. He understands me. He is there to hold my hand 24/7. The love that He showers on us is indescribable, and there is really no one like Him.

◆ **Text by Felicia Chin**

Faith

"There is no safe place in Afghanistan." She went anyway

A Unicef photo of Afghan children displaced by war.

AFGHANISTAN 2018

January 24: "The car bombing and gun attack took place at the office of international charity Save the Children."

January 27: "An ambulance rigged with explosives killed at least 103 people in Kabul, most of them civilians."

March 19: "A motorcycle bomb exploded near a political rally at a football stadium."

May 31: "Today's bombing in a crowded area of central Kabul was yet another reminder of how deadly the war has become for ordinary Afghan civilians."

August 15: "The explosion was in a Shia neighbourhood which prepares students for university exams."

3. 103. 4. 15. 34.
Dead.
Dead.
Dead.
"Pain deepens for Afghanistan."
"No one should see such a day."
"There is no safe place in Afghanistan."

SINGAPORE 2018

"Hello? Hello?"

A girl's soft voice comes over the crackling line.

"Can you hear me?" I am almost shouting into my phone.

"Hang on," she says. "I'm trying to get a good signal. Let me make my way to the roof. Maybe the reception is better there."

Footsteps on stone. *Pap, pap, pap.* A sudden sense of open air.

"Can you hear me?" she says, her voice unexpectedly clear now.

We were supposed to skype – the alchemy of the internet allowing two women 5,144km apart to talk "face to face" – me in Singapore, R* in Afghanistan.

But the electricity went off an hour ago, R apologises, and her computer is dead. *Can we just talk on the phone?*

I picture R on a flat Afghan rooftop overlooking an organic warren of brown-bricked homes, the sounds of market nearby, the Hindu Kush mountains soaring in the misty distance, her *chador* headscarf blowing in an arid breeze as she holds up her phone to "catch" the reception.

What could possess a Singapore girl to live in a place so far removed from home – where young children are familiar with the smell of bomb smoke, armed security posts block your way to work, and women exist under cultural conditions so extreme that the place has been repeatedly named "the most dangerous country for women" by gender-issue experts?

For R, there is only one answer: God.

FROM NUS TO NGO

R became a believer at age 14.

"Early in my faith, during secondary school, I was going to Thailand with my church and I felt something click," says R, now 33. "Singapore is the Antioch of Asia and I wanted to be a part of Singapore's prophecy."

"I thought they were crazy! I didn't even know of any Singaporean in Afghanistan!"

In university, R was active in a Christian varsity group.

"We shared the love of God with the students, staff and cleaners on campus and they came to the faith. Looking back, God was preparing me to serve Him in the nations."

The varsity group organised summer trips to Central Asia and R found herself on a short trip to Kyrgyzstan, where she stayed with a local family.

Sharing that they felt strongly called to Afghanistan, the couple invited R to go with them to babysit their three boys, who at the time were just five, three and less than a year old.

"When they asked me, I thought they were crazy!" recalls R. "This was 2009 – I didn't even know of any Singaporean in Afghanistan!"

But God had a plan.

THE ROAD TO AFGHANISTAN

Riots broke out in the south of Kyrgyzstan and R and her team were asked to leave immediately before the airports were shut down.

"We took the first available flight out of Bishkek (the capital of Kyrgyzstan) and it was going to Istanbul," recalls R. "On that flight, I happened to sit next to an Afghan man.

"This was the first Afghan face I would see in my life. To my surprise, he was very interested when I shared my faith.

"When we parted, he left me a note in his Persian language that said: *Afghanistan is a beautiful country. Please come to Afghanistan.*

"I was shocked. This was like a call from within. I felt God speak to my heart and I asked Him for confirmation."

"I told God, 'How can I go to the other side of the world if my own family does not know You?'"

In His grace, God provided a series of clear signs. The one R treasured most had to do with her family.

"I was the first believer in my family and I had told God, 'How can I go to the other side of the world if my own family does not know You?'

"Just before I was to leave for Kabul, my dad came to me and told me he wanted to get baptised.

"I thought he was going senile," she says with a laugh. "I had been sharing the Good News with my parents for 14 years before this! I put my parents in Alpha class and they encountered God very powerfully. My mum had a dramatic transformation in her life."

A VISION

In August 2010, R took a pivotal trip to Afghanistan.

She had just graduated from university and was serving out her scholarship.

"There were significant events prior to my arrival in Afghanistan. A medical team that was in the country to administer healthcare was ambushed and killed.

"When I arrived in Kabul, I felt like an outsider, but I felt privileged, too, to be part of a sacred time of grieving.

"God really challenged me – and I still feel constantly challenged – on what it means to live for Him and maybe even lose my life for my faith."

"I feel constantly challenged on what it means to live for Him and maybe even lose my life for my Him."

R was visiting NGOs to study their work, "and also figure out what work God was calling me to do".

If she had any lingering doubts she was meant to be in Afghanistan, they were laid to rest when God gave her a powerful vision.

"We were travelling to the central mountainous province of Bamyan. At the time, there was no airport there."

Bamyan is beautiful, remembers R. It is the cultural capital of the Hazara ethnic group, descendants of Mongols.

"We were travelling by car to this beautiful lake which was about a two-hour journey and I was staring out of the window at the desert. It was hot.

"All at once, I had a vision of a big, fierce man in a turban. In his hands was an AK47 rifle and he was running towards me.

"He was shouting in a language I didn't understand. I was really scared.

"But when he was close enough, about two metres away, I realised he had tears in his eyes. And I found that I could understand what he was saying.

"When he came closer, he fell on his knees and cried out, *'Tell me, tell me – what must I do to be saved?'"*

Shaken, R realised that God was showing her the spiritual condition of His people in Afghanistan.

"That really broke my heart ... we read about evil terrorists in the news. But they are not always evil, they are *desperate*. Now even when attacks happen, I see them in a different light."

BLASTS AND GUNFIRE

Still, the danger is palpable.

As we speak, R is living in the aftermath of an ambulance suicide attack that took the lives of over 100 civilians and injured more than 235.

She happened to be in Delhi during the attack on Saturday. On Sunday, she was determinedly back in Kabul.

Returning to her home from the airport, she could still hear blasts and gunfire.

Returning to her home from the airport, she could still hear blasts and gunfire.

She was on lockdown for a few days and then was relegated to "essential movement", meaning movement was restricted to going to work and straight back home.

"Life goes on," says R simply. "This is how Afghans deal with it … just carry on."

As a security measure, she has to move residences quite often, she says.

It was actually a year ago when I first heard R speak about her work in Afghanistan. At the time, she was back in Singapore on home leave.

As she shared, the alarm on her phone split the silence in the small hall, making the listeners jump.

"Sorry," she apologised with a smile. "It's my daily reminder to call my organisation's security officer."

That's when it hit me – this young woman was living in such treacherous circumstances that she had standing instructions to call her organisation every evening, failing which they'd get the alert: *R is in danger*.

Suddenly the tranquility with which she was speaking about the beauty of Afghanistan cut a stark contrast to her perilous mission for God.

THE REAL HEROES

It is now R's third year working for NGOs in Afghanistan.

Having taken local language lessons, she works on community development projects with disabled children, and conducts maternal health training (essential in a country where infant mortality rates are among the highest in the world), water sanitation talks and small business training.

"Our local Afghan staff work directly with our beneficiaries. My role is more monitoring and evaluating the projects, and giving training. The locals are the real heroes.

"I'm very proud of my staff – there is good work being done by the Afghans for the Afghans," R says warmly.

There are 73 ethnic groups in Afghanistan, she explains, the main group being Pashtun.

"But I look Hazara," she adds. "So I blend in. I think it's God's preparation for me – it gives me access to many places. I still have to wear a *burqa* in certain areas, but my skin colour is the same as theirs. It's a privilege – I can move about quite freely as compared to my western colleagues."

In a country where "there is no safe place", the expat community is understandably small, and whoever has remained has become a family of sorts ... making it grimly personal when one of their own is kidnapped. Or worse.

"It shocked me to discover that they kidnap foreigners and sell them to the Taleban as bargaining chips."

Last year, a "sister" who had given 12 years of her life to the Afghans, was killed.

A friend, who was to be her roommate, was also kidnapped last year.

"We kept praying for our kidnapped friend and finally she was released.

"Security and governance are low, unemployment rates are high, the country is unstable, and people are desperate. It shocked me to discover that it is a common strategy to kidnap foreigners and sell them to the Taleban as bargaining chips.

"That shook me and my friends. It makes faith real, especially when we talk about new earth and new heaven and new Jerusalem. Until then, we are called to patiently endure," she says soberly.

When R first started working in Afghanistan, there were about 120 expats, an international school and community centre.

At the time we spoke, R was one of fewer than 10 left in her organisation, and the international school and community centre had closed.

I HEAR THEM PRAY

"Life here is a constant stress and it accumulates," confesses R. "You hear blasts and gunfire daily.

"For me personally, it was almost a tipping point last year. I went back to Singapore and stayed for three and a half months. I had post traumatic stress disorder (PTSD) counselling and debriefing. I 'offloaded' as much as possible so I could go back to Afghanistan and serve another term.

"It becomes a rhythm – my counsellor helps me process, and I continue to do the work God has called me to do.

"The believers are few but growing, weak but strong. *I look at Afghanistan and I hear them pray.*"

"One of my leaders has been in Afghanistan for 21 years and she is still convicted to stay.

"When you look at the work that remains to be done in this place ... it would take a lifetime. But I take it a term at a time. And I try to listen to God."

Recently R attended a conference in India for workers in the Persian world.

Still shaken by the kidnapping and killing of her friends, she told God: "I don't know how much I can do when I'm in this state."

"And God reassured me about a new season. He kept speaking to me about water breaking through and walls coming down. This was confirmed by many others in the community.

"When we returned to Afghanistan, we saw people coming to the faith and it was just incredible.

"We boldly prayed and this girl was healed. God was moving. To see this young woman, saying in response to killing and blasts among her own people, that we were on the right track and Satan was not happy ... I was so encouraged.

"The believers are few but growing, weak but strong. *I look at Afghanistan and I hear them pray.*"

COMING HOME

She is back on home leave every year – but it is surprisingly difficult to come home.

"You can't be comfortable here when your friends' lives are endangered. You can't," says R, who now feels more comfortable with people like older pastors, who understand grief and loss.

"For people my age, there is often no concept of pain or grief or loss on a regular basis."

"Every time I say goodbye to my family, they cry and I cry. This has made us really cherish the time we have together."

She has a group of close girlfriends who grew up together.

"I spent the first 26 years of my life in Singapore. But I sometimes find it hard to relate to my friends now," she says quietly.

"When I first came home and I was still traumatised, I would get angry with them when they talked about things that didn't matter to me. I was almost swearing and I was shocked at myself.

"But my friends allowed me to be who I am. They bore everything up to the point I had to leave again, and then they cried and told me, 'Don't go. It's hard for us to pray to God, *Your will be done*, knowing you could be killed.

"I tell them, 'It's okay. It's the same when I pray for my Afghan friends. I say, *Oh God, don't let them be hurt*.

"So we meet at that level and I'm thankful for my friends and I accept their love gratefully."

It is even harder with family.

"Every time I go back to Afghanistan and say goodbye to my family, they cry and I cry, and it's emotional. This has made us, as a family, really cherish the time we have together.

"I think they still wish that I would come home, but they are proud of me and I'm very proud of them, because they understand and are supportive of what I do. And that's very important to me."

CLOSER TO HEAVEN

Hard as life is in Afghanistan, R is anything but dark.

She chatters about bringing Afghan cashews, walnuts, pine nuts and almonds – "good stuff!" – back for her mum and stocking up on *Wang Wang* crackers, *bak kwa* and salted egg yolk potato chips when she returns to Afghanistan.

"I'm still a Singaporean," she laughs.

She turned 33 in Afghanistan this March. You can hear the smile in her voice as she tells you: "My birthday is a holiday here.

"It's a very happy time, a beautiful time of the year when the farmers sow seeds, and I'm thankful that my birthday is the first day of spring."

Does she think about dating and marriage like other Singaporean girls?

"You know, I used to think about it and ask God, 'So will I get married?'

"But marriage, to me, is a luxury. Staying alive is a priority. Who knows if I will be alive next week or next year?

"Marriage is a luxury. Staying alive is a priority. Who knows if I will be alive next week or next year?"

"In the light of eternity, I have no regrets at all.

"The reality of us as pilgrims in a passing world is very real here. Honestly, I feel closer to heaven.

"Singapore is like a bubble; there aren't even 'basic' things like natural disasters! What is faith if we go to church and say, 'God is good because He gave me a bonus'?

"Afghanistan is a place that confronts you. Here, basic things don't work – electricity, heating – so you just have to cry out to God and depend on Him."

And life is not all doom and gloom.

"There are also good things and funny things," she says. "Last week a horrid attack happened. And a group of demonstrators wanted to burn the Pakistan flag outside the embassy. But many here are illiterate and they burned the Nigerian flag by mistake! An officer had to apologise to Nigeria. It was just so crazy and funny … it only happens in Afghanistan!"

Even if she wants to stay in Afghanistan, she doesn't know how long she will be allowed to, as aid workers may be asked to leave if there is a major incident.

"So every day is a privilege," she says, her voice a prayerful hush.

"In a place like this, evil is sometimes right in your face. But I remember John 1:5: *The light shines in the darkness, and darkness has not overcome it*."

◆ **Text by Juleen Shaw**

Editor's Note: R's name has been withheld for security reasons.

"Go home, leave now!" Lebanese pastor felt "inexplicable prompting" to close refugee centre hours before explosion

At the Life Center, which Ps Said has invested 11 years into, doors were blown off their hinges, ceilings had fallen, windows and glass panels were shattered. Lights, air conditioners, computers and laptops were destroyed. Photo courtesy of Ps Said.

"Shock after shock, after shock, after shock. People are traumatised. What's next?" 53-year-old Pastor Said Deeb, the Director of Life Center Lebanon, told *Salt&Light* in a phone interview from Beirut.

The turmoil in Lebanon is escalating. After massive explosions in Beirut on Tuesday, August 4, 2020, the Lebanese Cabinet resigned amidst rising public anger yesterday (August 10).

It is the latest development in a country which has experienced a revolt, economic and financial crises caused by hyperinflation and currency devaluation, and widespread food shortages.

Ps Said admitted: "When you see everything destroyed. People committing suicide because of hunger … Sometimes, we lose heart.

"You need to face it by courage and faith – or surrender."

"PROMPTING" SAVES 34

"I don't know what it was but God spared our lives," Ps Said told *Salt&Light*. "My people asked, 'Pastor, how did you know about the explosion?' It was a miracle."

The Lebanese pastor runs a humanitarian relief centre for refugees in Beirut located just over 1 mile (1.6 km) from the port of Beirut where almost 3,000 tonnes of ammonium nitrate exploded, damaging buildings as far as 10 miles (16 km) away.

On a regular day, the four-storey Life Center is bustling with church meetings, a school for refugee children, discipleship classes and even a food kitchen in the basement.

But late Tuesday morning, Ps Said felt an inexplicable prompting to stop all the meetings, cancel all activities and close the centre.

"I had a feeling. So, 34 people, I sent them all home."

"All of you, go home! Leave now," he told everyone present. "Don't come back until Sunday for church."

"I was rude. I don't know if it was the Lord, but I had a feeling. So, 34 people, I sent them all home," recalled Ps Said, adding that it was a "heavy" feeling.

For himself, however, it was a double intervention. When Ps Said left the church office to run an errand at the port, he was told to return the next day because the paperwork he needed was not ready.

He left just after noon, stopping to deliver lunch to a group of Nigerian believers who had been left unemployed and stranded

"God spared our lives," said Pastor Said, whose move to cancel all meetings and activities at the refugee relief centre saved the lives of 34 people that day. Photo courtesy of Pastor Said Deeb.

after the Covid shutdown and left to meet another pastor in his home, a 40-minute drive south of the port.

Ps Said was there praying together when the explosion occurred at 6.08pm. When he saw the breaking news, Ps Said was alarmed. His mother and two aunts lived in an apartment in the exact neighbourhood.

"I started calling people – my wife, children, everyone. But the lines were so busy, I couldn't connect to anyone," Ps Said recounted. He rushed back to the city as WhatsApp messages on the various groups started coming in.

Over text, he soon found out that his wife and four children, as well as everyone from the Life Center, were alive and well. (It was only at 2am, more than eight hours later, that Ps Said found out his mother and aunts had been injured and were transported unconscious to a nearby hospital for treatment.)

Because of Ps Said's action that afternoon, the lives of the 34 people at the centre that day were preserved.

ROADS COVERED WITH GLASS

"It was smoke and panic everywhere. It was disastrous," Ps Said recalled. "Cars had no windows. Rocks, metals and glass on the roads – I drove for kilometres over glass."

Beirut's governor, Marwan Abboud, estimates that up to US$15 billion worth of damage has been done and over 300,000 homes are damaged, many left uninhabitable. Photo courtesy of Pastor Chady El-Aouad.

When Ps Said eventually reached Life Center, he stared at the destruction in dismay.

> "Cars had no windows. Rocks, metals and glass on the roads – I drove for kilometres over glass."

The doors had been blown off their hinges, ceilings had fallen, windows and glass panels had shattered. The lights, air conditioners, computers and laptops were destroyed.

The Life Center, which he had invested 11 years into, was already in dire need of funds before the explosion, the cost of repairs now would be beyond their means. (Because of hyperinflation and economic crisis, bank accounts have been frozen and only fresh funds can be withdrawn).

Ps Said knew they needed to get to work.

"The whole night, we were at the church cleaning the rubbish and protecting it," he said. Local gangs were already mobilised to take advantage of the chaos and were stealing from unoccupied shops and houses.

For two days and two nights, staff and volunteers helped to clean up the Life Centre and stayed to make sure that the premises

For two days and two nights, staff and volunteers helped to clean up the Life Centre and stayed to make sure that the premises were not looted. Photo courtesy of Ps Said Deeb, Life Centre.

were not looted. Some were refugees who left their homes unguarded to help clean up Life Centre, located in Beirut's low-income and red light district. By late Thursday night, they had cleared out the debris and Ps Said went home to sleep for the first time since the blast on Tuesday evening.

REFUGEES RETURN TO HELP

"The Syrian refugees, they came to help us," Ps Said, adding that a Syrian teenager, Youssef, who had been taken in and cared for by the staff and volunteers of Life Center, had even left his little apartment damaged while he helped out.

People were asking after one another, showing affection and love in action, even sharing tears.

When Ps Said found out, he called Youssef aside and asked him to go home. But Youssef refused, saying: "The house of God is more important than my house."

"I was crying," Ps Said exclaimed. "I felt God's presence; He is with us! My faith was stirred. We are not going to surrender."

By Thursday morning, over 30 of them had cleared the centre of the dust and debris, taking turns to keep watch through Tuesday and Wednesday night. And Ps Said sent several youth to help Youssef clean up the debris in his home.

Others spread out into the neighbourhood to help out and distribute sandwiches to those cleaning the streets and damaged apartments. The centre barely had cash to spare, but Ps Said felt prompted to feed those in need around the church and others who were helping with the clean-up in the community.

Refugees and youth of the Church of God, Ps Said's church which meets on the premises, took to the streets to distribute sandwiches and offer help to those in need. Photo courtesy of Ps Said Deeb.

Refugees and youth of the Church of God, Ps Said's church which meets on the premises, took to the streets to distribute sandwiches and offer help to those in need. They did this in faith, knowing that Life Centre itself, was running low on cash.

He said: "My team was working and refugees were cleaning and helping other people – we started reaching out, helping and giving to others. This is Jesus. He was bruised, suffering on the Cross, but at the same time, He was giving us life."

"We have hope and smiles to give – and hope brings faith, which is all that counts in times like this."

Actions like this were forthcoming from all directions.

Churches from outside Beirut had started calling him, offering to send teams to help with the clean-up and messages of support and financial assistance were coming in from around the world.

People were asking after one another, showing affection and love in action, even sharing tears, Ps Said commented. "I thought, wow, when suffering happens, people unite. For me, this is everything about Christianity.

"Everything," he emphasised.

BY FAITH ALONE

While the premises are free of debris, Ps Said estimated that he will need close to 50,000USD (S$70,000) to restore the Life Centre. He does not know where or when the funds will reach him, but efforts are underway in countries like the UK, Switzerland and Singapore.

"By faith, we started. By faith, we will continue."

While funds are needed, Ps Said is seeking prayer as well. "The most important thing now is to pray for us," he said.

"Boldness. Courage. To continue reaching and serving the community. You need boldness when you go to help people and you don't have anything to help them.

"We are like Peter and John who said, 'Silver and gold we have none'. But we have hope and smiles to give – and hope brings faith, which is all that counts in times like this.

"By faith, we started. By faith, we will continue."

◆ **Text by Tan Huey Ying**

Faith

"It had to be the Lord": Former national swimmer Joscelin Yeo on her life's dramatic turnaround

After a devastating miscarriage, Joscelin "held on to God's Word and His promise to me that children are my inheritance. (Psalm 127:3) An inheritance is something you don't earn. It's something that you're given." She now has four children. Photos from Joscelin Yeo's Facebook page.

Joscelin Yeo will always be remembered as one of Singapore's golden girls. In the 1990s, she flew the Singapore flag high at regional swimming meets. Her name resounded from television sets across the island and was splashed across news headlines as she made waves in the pool.

Joscelin Yeo's international swimming career began when she was 11 years old at the 1990 Asian Games. She retired in 2007 after a 17-year competitive swimming career.

Her record haul of 40 gold medals in the Southeast Asian Games remains unchallenged.

But for Yeo, her competition days are mostly water under the bridge now. "Achievements come and go, they don't make up who I am.

"Being a swimmer is something that people identify me with. It's something I did out of routine but it is not who I am on the inside."

"NO WAY IT COULD BE COINCIDENCE"

At age 11, she was the fastest breaststroker and made the national team. Thus began a career of 17 years as a national swimmer.

But lurking beneath the surface of the bemedalled young athlete was a troubled teen.

"There was no way of escape and I felt like my life was a complete toilet bowl."

"While it was fun being on the national team, I was exposed to a lot of things that I wouldn't have normally be exposed to at that age," she shared. "I had to face the media constantly. I couldn't go anywhere without being seen or being asked to do something. I just had no privacy. And it was really hard, especially as I was going through my teenage years.

"I ended up turning to partying, smoking, drinking as a way of escape and it just got worse and worse and worse each year. I did every kind of vice that you can probably think of.

"I spiralled into depression, I cut myself to try and get away from internal turmoil. There was no way of escape and I felt like my life was a complete toilet bowl."

Her life turned around as a young adult when, to spend time with her brother, she went along with him to church.

> "There's no way it could be so coincidental ... It really had to be the Lord."

"Even though I went, I fell asleep very early on because I was completely hungover. But towards the end of the service (at the altar call) I just felt compelled to raise my hand up. I think it was when I felt the compulsion to raise my hand that I felt that hope that well, maybe, maybe, if I accept Christ, my life could turn around. I didn't know for sure, but I think at that point my life was so bad that I was willing to try anything.

"This is where it's so beautiful because the Lord had already provided a way out for me. I had actually been getting calls from coaches in the States offering me full scholarships to go over there to swim ... it provided me a way out, a fresh start, a new beginning.

"There's no way it could be so coincidental that everything came together at that point. It really had to be the Lord."

GRACE TO HEED THE CALL

Today, at 40 years of age, the shine comes from within, from a life surrendered.

For the last 13 years, Yeo has been on staff with New Creation Church. She started out in the youth ministry where, for the self-confessed introvert, was not exactly the best fit. "I had to overcome a lot of anxiety. Being in front of the crowd is something that I'm not naturally comfortable with."

Joscelin celebrating her big 4-0 in May 2019, flanked by her family. Her children are very active and have different bents, "so I'll let them move into whichever area they enjoy. There's a lot of value in sports, so I would like for them to do some kind of sport. If it's swimming, then swimming. If it's not, it's not. But not competitive sport, they are a bit too young for that," she says.

> "I believed that, where the Lord had called me, there would be a supply of grace and ability."

But as a competitive swimmer, Yeo had been trained to stay the course. The prize was of a high calling (Philippians 3:14).

"I was given the opportunity, I just took it by faith and stepped into it," she said.

"It's about being willing to do, and go, where God has called me to. And also believing that, where the Lord has called, there will be a supply of grace and ability."

Yeo warmed up to the role and bonded well with the youth. At her wedding in 2010, wedding photographer Gilbert Chua commented that the wedding couple was "well loved" by the youths in the church.

The youths turned up in droves for Joscelin Yeo's wedding in 2010. Picture courtesy of 9Frames.

After six years of working with the youth, Yeo moved to her church's counselling ministry where she now serves in a part-time role.

> "I meditated on that truth until it became so evident that there was no two ways about it."

Even though she has put her swimming days behind her, Yeo admits that competitive training has provided her with lessons of perseverance.

"But without God all that couldn't have come into play, because after a while, you just get tired and emotions always get the better of you.

"That resilience is also about hunkering down and saying, 'God's Word says this so I'm going to hold on, stand firm, until I see that truth comes to pass in my life.'

"Resilience with faith, coupled together, helped me."

JUST ENOUGH MANNA

Yeo paused for a moment when asked to share a time when she had to exercise both resilience and faith.

"My first pregnancy I miscarried," she shared very quietly.

"It's not something you expect when you're pregnant. So that was really tough and we were grieving."

"I don't have answers to why it happened.

"But I just held on to God's Word and His promise that children are my inheritance (Psalm 127:3), the fruit of my womb is my reward. I kept holding on to the verses – an inheritance is something you don't earn. It's something that you're given.

"I meditated on that truth until it became so evident that there was no two ways about it – *children are my inheritance*."

Her faith and trust were not misplaced.

Sean, her eldest child, arrived in due course, and soon after, three others followed.

Joscelin Yeo and Joseph Purcell have been married for nine years. Purcell serves as a full-time pastor in their church.

Joscelin's children, each bearing a special 40th birthday gift for their mum. Sarah (*front left*) is the youngest, while Sean (*front right*) will be 9 at the end of the year. David (*back left*), is 7, while Michael (*back right*) is 5.

GIVING BACK

There is even a bigger brood that she takes care of as the Vice-President (Swimming) of the Singapore Swimming Association.

"I love the sport. It's something that I was involved in with for many years as an athlete. It is something that I can give back to the community in terms of my experience. I want to help the sport grow and give athletes better support to achieve their dreams," said Yeo.

"The Bible says there's enough manna for each day, so there's grace enough for each day."

How does she wear so many caps and yet manage to keep her head above water?

"The Bible says there's enough manna for each day (Exodus 16:4-12), so there's grace enough for each day," said the former Nominated Member of Parliament.

"If I sat down and talked about the zillion things that I need to do in the next one week, I probably would just freeze because I don't think I'd be able to do it. But if I just take one thing at a time, and one day at a time, there's grace enough for each day.

"If there's something that I need to be aware of, I trust the Lord to highlight it to me. And I get that done first.

"In Romans 5:17, it says: 'For if, because of one man's trespass, death reigned through that one man, much more will those who receive the abundance of grace and the free gift of righteousness reign in life through the one man Jesus Christ.'

"This is a truth that speaks volumes to me. If that were not true, I would not be where I am today."

◆ **Text by Karen Tan**

Faith

Three children with fatal genetic disorder, yet David Lang sees God's sovereignty

Singapore Bible College lecturer David Lang, 60, is the father of two children struck with a rare genetic disorder called Niemann-Pick Disease Type C. The disease causes the patient's physical and intellectual functions to deteriorate over time. Photo by Rachel Phua.

David Lang is a surprisingly chatty man, despite the heartache that encircles him. As the tunes from a children's television show hum in the background, Lang talks about the theology of suffering at the dining table.

But first, he apologises profusely for forgetting about the interview, before he makes a spurt around his home, a spartan five-room flat along Farrer Road, to get ready.

The 60-year-old, who won the Extraordinaire Caregiver Award this March, is a lecturer at the Singapore Bible College, his alma mater. Yet these days, academic pursuits have taken a backseat for the father of two (it used to be three).

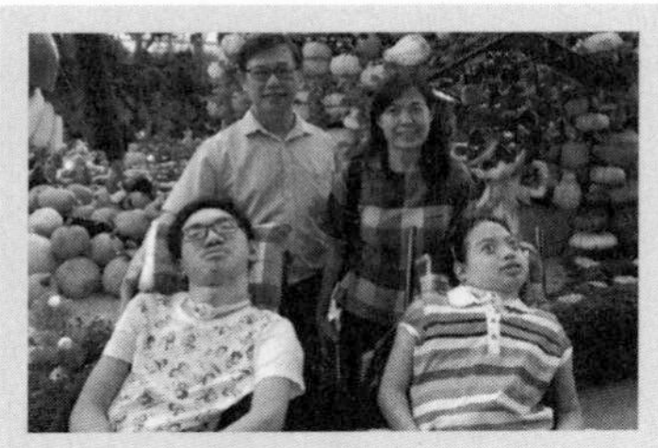

Lang and his wife take their children out for walks around their block every evening. On weekends and public holidays, the couple take their children out to local attractions like Gardens by the Bay and Chinatown. Photo courtesy of David Lang.

His two surviving children, Justina, 27, and Titus, 21, both have Niemann-Pick Disease Type C, a rare and fatal genetic disorder that has caused their intellectual and physical faculties to weaken. There is currently no cure for it, and there are only about 500 diagnosed cases worldwide. Lang believes his children are the first known cases in Singapore.

Though born healthy, they are now paralysed and and unable to speak. Both of them are bedridden, tube-fed, and require a ventilator to breathe. As the older child, Justina is almost fully paralysed, to the point where she is unable to move her head or control her eye movements.

To look after them, Lang made special arrangements with the college so that he does not have to observe office hours. His wife, Loo Geok, 59, teaches Hebrew occasionally at the school while she takes care of the children full-time, alongside their two helpers. Justina and Titus require round-the-clock care, even when they are asleep – Lang and Loo Geok get up every three hours to clear their kids' secretions.

FACING HEARTBREAK

Naturally, Lang dug deep into Scripture at the beginning of his ordeal. When he and his wife identified their children's condition, it was more than six years after Justina first showed symptoms of the disease.

By the time she was 13, Justina had been transferred from doctor to doctor, misdiagnosed with cerebral palsy at one point and put on a variety of drugs to control her seizures.

The death of Lang's second child, Timothy, was what led to the discovery.

It was June 2004. By then, Timothy was already displaying early signs of Niemann-Pick, acting up uncontrollably and having difficulty swallowing. One morning at breakfast during church camp in Johor, he choked on a piece of bacon before it could be cut up.

A church member who was a doctor tried to perform a Heimlich manoeuvre, but Timothy went into a seizure, making it impossible. He was turning blue as his family rushed him to the local hospital.

After 19 days in coma, Timothy died on July 19 2004, a month before his 11th birthday.

Lang recalls Timothy's childhood. His son was a "brilliant" and "almost perfect" boy, he says. His family now jokes that Timothy was sanctified ahead of everyone else, which was why God took him home first.

Timothy with his mum. Photo courtesy of David Lang.

Timothy was a keen learner who loved to read and try new things. Lang brought his family to science museums frequently while living in the US, and Timothy would read all the information on the panels though his dad thought they were too complex for his age. He was never shy to introduce himself to other children either, or display his affections.

"Till today, I cry when I think of my son."

"One of the things Timothy liked to do in primary school was to take the money we gave him for recess to buy something for me," Lang reminisces. "He would buy a marker saying, 'Daddy, I give this to you'.

Titus (*left*) and Timothy (*right*). Lang says Titus was badly affected by his elder brother's death, and he became very quiet after Timothy's death. Photo courtesy of David Lang.

"I'd tell him, 'This is money for you to eat at school'. But the next time he would present me with a sharpener or an eraser.

"Till today, I cry when I think of my son."

Meanwhile, Justina's ailment was still a mystery among the doctors the family met, until her neurologist sent Timothy's tissue samples to a research laboratory in the US that focused on rare diseases among adolescence. Subsequent tests showed that all three of Lang's kids were afflicted.

SEARCHING FOR ANSWERS

Lang says he and Loo Geok went through different stages of grief throughout the entire process – denial, anger, bargaining, depression, eventually acceptance.

Like Job, Lang cried out to God: "Why me?" (Job 7:20) during the initial years. He was angry with God. Why would a loving Father allow innocent children to suffer?

There was pressure on the couple to find the right treatment for their children: Put them on experimental therapy? Go for healing rallies? The pair often quarrelled with each other at the beginning, going to bed in tears, Lang says.

Like Job's friends, some of the couple's acquaintances, while well meaning, added to their burden.

"Now, I will just wait on the Lord."

"One of the problems we faced in the first two years of our daughter's degeneration was people telling us, 'The reason your children are not healed is because you lack faith.'

"I told them, 'I believe God can heal, and I have asked that my children be healed. Now, I will just wait on the Lord.'"

Lang with his children during their early days. Photo courtesy of David Lang.

"They told me, 'No, you have to be like the persistent widow (Luke 18:1-8). Keep going for rallies the way she went to the judge until God decides to heal them.'"

Lang began to question his faith, so he restudied the passage. "It refers to the justice God will bring, not answered prayers. It's about the second coming."

FINDING SOLACE IN JOB

To cope, Lang dove into the book of Job, which brought immense comfort at times when he felt guilty for his outrage towards God.

"As a bible college lecturer, who am I to question God. Was I a hypocrite? I even thought of resigning," he says.

> "I have heard of You by the hearing of the ear, but now my eye sees You." (Job 42:5)

"But then Job also spoke against God. And God didn't fault him. His response was: 'Job has spoken of me what is right' (Job 42:7)."

Lang saw the beauty of God's sovereignty as well, in Job 38-39, when God finally answered Job through a long spiel of rhetorical questions. Some interpret it as God's rebuke of Job, but Lang found compassion and grace in God's words. He is in control over all existence.

And like the carefree ostrich (Job 39:13-18) and the wilful horse (Job 39:19-25), God was going to give the Lang family the joy and courage to trudge on amidst the pain.

THERE YOU ARE, GOD

Lang saw his children degenerate in front of his own eyes, his young son die, his savings plummet. But he had found his answer in one of Job's final words in the chapter:

I have heard of You by the hearing of the ear,
But now my eye sees You (Job 42:5 NKJV).

Because of his suffering, Job felt the very presence of the God he yearned for.

Because of his suffering, Job felt the very presence of God he yearned for (Job 23:3). Lang was never this close to the Redeemer until his children arrived.

"Actually, it was through Timothy's death that I found peace with our children's condition. When Timothy was in a coma, there was a strange sense of peace within me that I can only attribute to God," he says, referencing Philippians 4:7.

Lang could finally shift his focus from this earthly life to the eternal hope he had.

Doctors were unable to detect Justina's condition until she was about 13, more than six years after symptoms started appearing. Photo courtesy of David Lang.

SHIELDED FROM THE FLAMES

At Timothy's funeral, Lang received a vision. In it, he and his family were caught in a fire, but a group of people was shielding them from the flames so they did not have to bear the full blast of the fire. He saw that his life was a gift from God, and the ability to undergo suffering was a community effort.

"When Timothy was in a coma, there was a strange sense of peace within me that I can only attribute to God."

Money is tight in their household. Lang takes home less than $5,000 a month, though monthly expenses hover between $7,000 to $9,000. They get by with help from their extended family, church members, strangers and the occasional crowdfunding campaign. A recent *The Sunday Times* article rallied his friends to help Lang raise more than $120,000 to replace one of his cars, a 28-year-old Toyota Corolla.

Others have come up to them during their walks to offer words of encouragement, which he does not take for granted.

These encounters have sometimes turned into opportunities to share about Christ, Lang adds. People would ask how he and Loo Geok cope, allowing them to slip into conversations the Gospel message.

THEY ARE GOD'S TREASURE

Midway during the interview, I ask a sensitive question: "What's going to happen to Justina and Titus after you and your wife pass away?"

Lang chuckles. "We'll probably outlive them," he answers matter of factly.

He has learnt to count his blessings. God has prolonged the life of both his daughter and his son, he says. Most people with the disease die between the ages of 10 and 25.

When Justina first needed a tracheostomy, a surgical procedure to create access for a breathing tube, one of the doctors Lang and his wife consulted was hesitant about the operation. While it would extend her life, it would also prolong her misery, the doctor told them.

The couple left the hospital undecided. Meanwhile, they continued to pump air manually into her nose using a resuscitator.

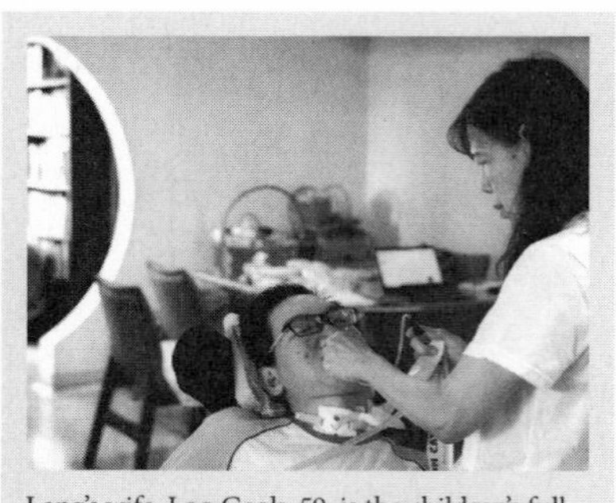

Lang's wife, Loo Geok, 59, is the children's full-time caretaker. Photo by Rachel Phua.

"There were times when we were pumping air into her and she would be smiling. One day I looked at my wife and said, 'I'm not ready to let her go'."

During the weekends, Lang and Loo Geok take their kids out to local attractions such as Gardens by the Bay and the Singapore Botanic Gardens to give them something to look forward to.

"At this age, they still go out with their parents. Which child still does that at their age," Lang jokes.

THIS ISN'T GOODBYE

"We will all meet again – in a place where there is no longer sickness, suffering or death."

Despite the optimism, Lang knows his children's final days are approaching, especially Justina's. Her condition has worsened significantly over the past two to three years, he says.

Lang is bracing himself. One thing he has learnt is not to hold on to his children too tightly, but to see them as God's treasure entrusted to them for the time being.

"Let me enjoy them while I can. I'll leave it to God when He finds it fit to take them home.

"This transient life will vanish one day. But we will all meet again – in a place where there is no longer sickness, suffering or death (Revelation 21:4)."

◆ **Text by Rachel Phua**

Faith

Falling into grace: What moral failure taught a reverend about God

Twenty-four hours was all it took for Rev Timothy Khoo's life to come crashing down. But "the exposure of my sin saved me from the duplicitous self that I had become", he revealed. Photo by Andrik Langfield on Unsplash.

"Nobody wants to be defined by the worst thing they've ever done. But on this side of heaven, that's often the case – the worst thing you've ever done defines you," Reverend Timothy Khoo quietly told a small crowd of about 50.

They had gathered to hear him share at an Eagles Leadership Conference 2019 masterclass entitled: *Recovering from Leadership Fallout and Moral Failure*.

Rev Khoo was sharing from his own experience.

"The real issue at the heart of my wrongdoing was wrong being; it was pride."

He was once a prominent preacher in one of the main denominations and the former president and CEO of Prison Fellowship International. But all of it was suddenly stripped away on August 30, 2014, following the public exposure of his sin. He had been involved in an inappropriate relationship.

He revealed that "it was significantly emotional; there were physical expressions ... but there was no sexual intercourse".

He did not say this to mitigate his guilt or the depravity of what he had done; quite the opposite. He reiterated that "sin is sin; adultery is infidelity by any standard". It is the standard set by Jesus: "You have heard that it was said, 'You shall not commit adultery.' But I say to you that everyone who looks at a woman with lustful intent has already committed adultery with her in his heart." (Matthew 5:27-28)

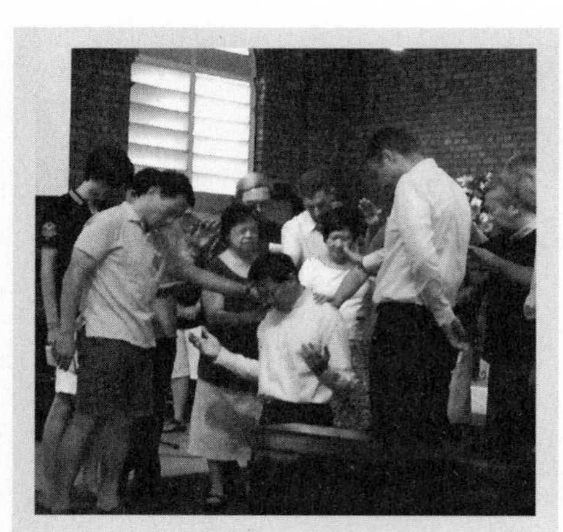

Rev Khoo, receiving prayer in his former home parish ahead of his installation as Prison Fellowship International's president and CEO in July 2013. Photo from Prison Fellowship International's Facebook page.

THE DUPLICITOUS MIND

"The duplicitous mind tried to rationalise that because – and I refrained from sexual intercourse for that very reason – I thought that in so doing, I would not be so wrong.

"You get my point? It was completely bogus, right?

"Because infidelity happened way before there was any physical contact. The betrayal happened way before there was any physical contact. But it was the mind that tried to believe that somehow it was not as bad," Rev Khoo, 54, said.

He referred to the *Confessions of St Augustine*, where the renowned theologian talked about two particular sins he had committed: One was that he fathered a child out of wedlock and the other was stealing pears from a neighbour's orchard.

The sin that bothered St Augustine more was the latter.

The child that he sired was conceived in genuine affection. Whereas his petty theft was done simply because he could get away with it.

"It was this endemic sin of pride, of believing that 'I can have what I want' without consequence," noted Rev Khoo.

"The real issue at the heart of my wrongdoing was wrong being; it was pride."

THE FALLACY OF INVINCIBILITY

"This is why leaders so often fail, because they think they're invincible," observed Rev Khoo. "They often think, I've attained this level of respect, responsibility, authority. I have earned the right to be president and CEO, pastor ... And I can do what I want and get away with it.

"I realised that there was a duality at play in my life, where I was living life on the surface in one way. But the life beneath the surface was somewhat – putting it mildly – different."

"I wore a mask and my face had grown to fit it."

Because of his status and position, he had lost himself. He had allowed his work to define him, instead of defining himself by who he was in Christ.

He recalled looking into the mirror on the fateful day he was publicly exposed. "I did not recognise the person staring back at me because the person that I was, up to that point, was all about my presidency and all about my priesthood. And all about the attendant accolades and affirmation.

With the local children in Swaziland during a Desert Odyssey journey. Photo from Desert Odyssey's Facebook page.

"I wore a mask and my face had grown to fit it," said Rev Khoo, drawing parallels to a George Orwell essay, *Shooting an Elephant*.

SEARING PAIN

"Twenty-four hours was all it took for everything to come crashing down. Did it save me from sin? Absolutely.

"It saved me from the duplicitous self that I had become," said Rev Khoo.

> "The exposure of my sin saved me from the duplicitous self that I had become."

The news devastated his wife, two teenaged sons and family, not to mention the parish and his colleagues. He still grieves about the hurt he caused them and the end of his marriage.

"Five years on, I'm still working through recovery," admitted Rev Khoo. After a year of church discipline, he was given the option to return to his posts.

But he turned them down "to allow God to mine the very depths of my heart, not just remove this sin but go deeper into the very depths of my heart".

He added: "It was a necessary, albeit very painful, process."

Close to a year after his ordeal, God's work in his life inspired him to start Desert Odyssey. He now organises spiritual retreats, where he guides participants on allowing God to mine the depths of their hearts in order to achieve healing and transformation.

"NOW YOU KNOW"

Rev Khoo never likened the way his life turned out to God punishing him. He recognised that this was the consequence of his sin. (Colossians 3:25, 1 Peter 2:20)

Days after everything imploded, he went cycling with his son. As he cycled, God began to speak: "For 25 years and two generations before, you've talked about shame, you've talked about guilt, vis-a-vis prisoners. You've talked about disappointing people you love to prisoners, letting people down, becoming the worst version of yourself.

"Now you know – shame, guilt, what it means to let people you love down, to break their hearts."

"But you had no clue what you were talking about because you had no experience of it ... when you talk to prisoners, it was all theoretical knowledge, theological constructs. Now you know – shame, guilt, what it means to let people you love down, to break their hearts."

Rev Khoo had to stop the bike as he broke down at those words as he recognised: "This is grace. This is God. This is redemption."

Then it dawned on him: "When Jesus died, He didn't say, 'I suffered so that you don't have to suffer.' Instead, 'I suffered so that your suffering will be like Mine.'

"In other words, it's a redemptive suffering. Not because He sinned, but because I did. I needed to suffer, I needed to feel every bit of the pain that I was feeling, every bit of the pain that people around me were feeling." (1 Peter 3:18)

"Even with the pain and sin of divorce, God still redeems," said Rev Khoo during the Eagles Leadership Conference 2019 in July. Photo courtesy of Eagles Communications.

REDEMPTIVE WORK OF THE CROSS

Losing his standing in the world was hard but nowhere as heart-breaking as losing his partner of almost 29 years to divorce.

Though the marriage was lost, God has restored their friendship. His ex-wife has also graciously extended a roof over Rev Khoo's head, something that he is immensely grateful for.

"I realised the restoration of the friendship was paramount. If something else follows after that, in terms of the restoration of marriage, I give thanks to God for that. But right now, it's this beautiful space of friendship," he said, his voice cracking.

"There is no justification for divorce – the Bible's very clear on it. But one of the redemptive outcomes of the divorce, by God's grace, was that my shadow was lifted from her. She was wilting under the shadow of my leadership.

"Even with the pain and sin of divorce, God still redeems."

ALL ABOUT GRACE

It has been a tough journey but, as Rev Khoo looks back, he sees nothing but the grace of God.

Yet there was a notion that he struggled with: "Whenever someone falls from some lofty position, whether in the secular world or in Christian organisations, we talk about a fall *from* grace."

> "I needed to suffer, to feel every bit of the pain that people around me were feeling."

He broached the topic with Friar John Wong from Order of Friars Minor, who provided him spiritual direction during that year of church discipline: "Help me understand this. I cannot wrap my mind around how I fell *from* grace. Because as I understand grace, I can't fall from it. Because grace is unmerited. So, what have I fallen from?" (Ephesians 2:8)

"Shouldn't we give thanks for our human nature, as broken as it is? Because we have inexplicably fallen not *from* grace, but we have undeservedly fallen *into* grace," replied Friar John.

"August 30, 2014, was the most dreadful, painful day of my life. But it was a day of grace," conceded Rev Khoo. He remembered the words from Brennan Manning's memoir, *All Is Grace*, that ministered to him during that bicycle ride:

"We have inexplicably fallen not *from* grace, but we have undeservedly fallen *into* grace."

Do you believe that the God of Jesus loves you beyond worthiness or unworthiness, beyond fidelity or infidelity – that He loves you in the morning sun and the evening rain – that He loves you when your intellect denies it, your emotions refuse it, your whole being rejects it. Do you believe that God loves without condition or reservation and loves you this moment as you are and not as you should be?

"He wants us to be the best, but He doesn't love us so that we can become the best. He loves us as we are, not as we should be. That is God, the unconditionality of God's love. And He knows that the freedom from sin allows us to be the best that we can become. But He doesn't love us because of that. He loves us in spite of that, He loves us as we are," reminded Rev Khoo.

"The message going out was the realisation of the weight of my sin. The revelation coming back is that all is grace. And so August 30, 2014, became for me, a day of grace."

◆ **Text by Geraldine Tan**

"God is alive, available and real": Pilot of last plane out of Palu before disaster hit

When he was airborne 1,500 feet (457m) above, Capt Ricoseta Mafella saw giant waves starting to form at the coastline. Screenshot from a video shot by Capt Mafella.

"The testimony of the Pilot of the last plane out of Palu before the earthquake." This was the title of the remarkable story that was flying around social media soon after the Palu, Sulawesi, earthquake and tsunami in 2019 that sent shock waves around the world.

In the testimony, the pilot, Captain Ricoseta Mafella from Batik Air, shared how he was inexplicably urged by the Holy Spirit to take off from Palu three minutes ahead of schedule.

> Did God really speak to him?

In so doing, Capt Mafella saved the 147 passengers and crew on his flight from certain danger.

"According to him, if he had taken off three minutes later, he would not have been able to save the 147 passengers and crew, because the asphalt on the landing strip was moving up and down like a curtain blowing in the wind," said the testimony which quickly went viral among Christian communities.

So was this a true story? Or was it – like so much on social media – fake news?

Salt&Light tracked down Capt Mafella to find out the truth: Did God really speak to him?

"BE QUICK"

Indeed, He did, said Capt Mafella.

"God calculated the process accurately," the veteran Batik Air pilot told *Salt&Light*. "The Holy Spirit was in control of my decision and of what I did."

> He heard the Holy Spirit tell him to "be quick, get out or depart quickly".

Capt Mafella, 44, is the pilot of the final plane that departed from Palu before the 7.5 magnitude earthquake and tsunami struck the Indonesian island of Sulawesi on September 29, at 18:02 local time.

According to the country's National Disaster Mitigation Agency, 2,256 people have died and another 1,309 were still missing.

After the twin disaster, Capt Mafella posted a tribute on his Instagram account, praising the air traffic controller Anthonius Gunawan Agung for sacrificing his life for the 147 passengers and crew on board the plane.

Agung was overseeing the plane's takeoff, which left the runway less than a minute before the earthquake hit.

He was in the control tower when it started shaking.

Unlike others in the building, Agung did not flee. He waited for the Batik Air flight to take off safely before jumping off the tower, which was collapsing by then.

Agung, 21, broke his arm, leg and ribs due to the plunge and died from his injuries.

"Batik 6231 runway 33 clear for take off" were Anthonius Gunawan Agung's last words.

Capt Mafella has been a pilot since 1993. Photo courtesy of Ricoseta Mafella.

His last words were: "Batik 6231 runway 33 clear for take off", wrote Capt Mafella on his Instagram post. There was no indication of panic in Agung's voice, he said.

The pilot told *Salt&Light* that, after he landed in Palu earlier in the afternoon and parked his aircraft, he heard the Holy Spirit tell him to "be quick, get out or depart quickly".

He got the crew to speed up the departure process for his flight leaving the island.

The passengers and crew had no clue of their close shave until much later.

NOT HIS FIRST NEAR-DEATH EXPERIENCE

The Palu disaster is just one of a few near-death experiences that the pilot of 25 years has been through, he said.

The incident has "strengthened me so much and proven that God is alive and available and real".

But this was the first time he felt immediate peace over the situation as he knew God was in control.

"I've been inside a church when it got bombed, I almost died because of dengue fever, and I was almost in a car crash before," he said. "The difference is death felt so imminent when they happened, and I was filled with fear.

"But with Palu, I faced it without fear."

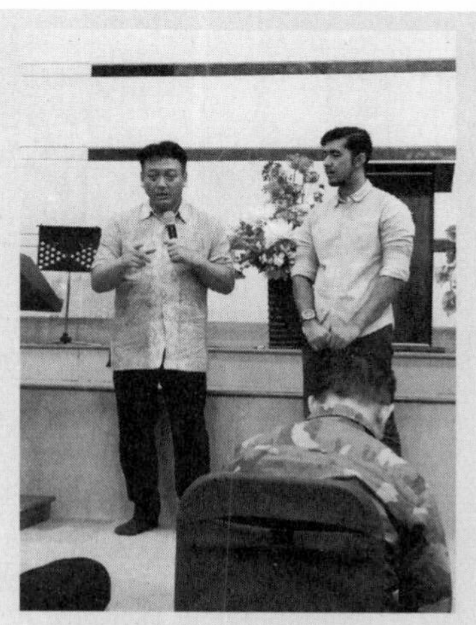

Capt Mafella and his co-pilot describing the flight out of Palu. Photo courtesy of Ricoseta Mafella.

Capt Mafella, a Christian from Jakarta, said that the incident has "strengthened me so much and proven that God is alive and available and real".

He added that Christians can pray for God's blessing and healing of the people in Palu, and that through His sustenance, they will come to Christ.

◆ **Text by Rachel Phua**

"Just love them": How the late Pastor Philip Chan became "Papa" to scores of troubled youths and their families

The Hiding Place family celebrating Ps Philip Chan's 69th birthday on January 7 this year. His love for all who pass through the doors of the halfway house has touched countless lives. Photo from Caleb Tan's Facebook.

"Just love them like they are family," the late Pastor Philip Chan said of over 1,000 men and their families who passed through the doors of The Hiding Place (THP), Singapore's first halfway house that he co-founded with his wife Christina.

Pastor Philip passed away at the age of 69 on February 3, 2020, after a battle with liver cancer.

After recovering from drug addiction and accepting the Lord on May 11, 1976, he began working with those struggling with drug addiction.

The home's motto, "As long as we live, we will open our door to anyone who knocks", is one that Ps Philip and his wife, Christina, took seriously from the start. They practised what they preached to their staff. (James 2:17)

This has seen them welcome not just drug addicts, but also ex-prisoners, gambling addicts, homeless orphans, troubled youths and anyone in need of help. This has even included those with mental disabilities.

The couple's radical love has touch countless lives, not just that of residents, but their families as well.

BIG HEARTEDNESS

Jenny Cheng was one those who was deeply impacted. She has known Ps Philip and Christina since 1987, when her brother, Sunny, first joined THP's residential rehabilitation programme. Sunny had been addicted to drugs since he was a teen and had been in and out of prisons.

Jenny Cheng (*left*) and her husband, Mike Tan (*right*), together with Ps Philip (*middle*) and Christina (*seated*). It was during her brother's time in The Hiding Place that Jenny got to know the Lord. Photo from Ps Philip Chan's Facebook.

Jenny recalled a time in 1992 when THP staff and residents were in Kuala Lumpur, Malaysia, for their church camp. Sunny received a call that his father was gravely ill. Without hesitation, Ps Philip purchased air tickets and accompanied Sunny back to Singapore.

"You see his love, you see God's love. Simple as that."

Sunny Cheng (*second from right*) with his parents and sister, Jenny, at The Hiding Place. It was through Ps Philip that they came to know the Lord. Photo courtesy of Jenny Cheng.

Despite Sunny's multiple stays in THP, he continued to struggle with drug addiction. His years of drug abuse finally caught up with him in 2011. When Ps Philip found out Sunny was in a hospital's intensive care unit, he rushed down to minister to him.

Ps Philip visited Sunny several times and it was during one of these visits that Sunny finally accepted Christ as his Lord and Saviour. He was eventually moved to a hospice to live out his remaining days.

Through Sunny's time at THP, both his parents and two of his siblings, including Jenny, came to know Christ. Jenny and her husband continue to attend the Corrie Ten Boom Centre, the church in THP's premises.

"Ps Philip told Sunny he could have his wake at THP. The only thing was, Ps Philip's birthday on January 7 may have fallen on the same day. He told Sunny that he could have his wake in the worship hall while he had his birthday celebration outside. Can you imagine this big-heartedness?" an emotional Jenny told *Salt&Light*. Her brother held on and died on January 8, 2011.

"That was the extent of Ps Philip's kindness to us, which was constantly and consistently shown throughout his life. You see his love, you see God's love. Simple as that."

A STUBBORN ROCK

When Kelvin Choo first set foot in THP in February 2017, he was adamant that he was just there to quit his drug addiction. Religion, to him, was secondary, having been brought up in a home where his dad was openly against Christianity.

> "Quitting substance abuse was actually a secondary problem. The primary problem was because I didn't have God in my life."

"Over time, I came to realise that quitting substance abuse was actually a secondary problem. The primary problem was because I didn't have God in my life," admitted Kelvin, 40, who accepted Christ nine months after being in THP.

As family visits were limited to once a fortnight, Kelvin's dad would take the opportunity to be see his son more frequently by attending the weekend church services held in THP. During that period, his dad was diagnosed with cancer.

"When my dad's condition worsened, THP made special arrangements for me to take him to hospital, to give us more time together. When he was unable to walk, the staff accompanied me home to have dinner with my family," Kelvin told *Salt&Light*.

"My dad was touched by these gestures and it was then that he decided to accept the Lord. I was really, really surprised. It was a very big miracle – seeing how God moved this stubborn rock," he said, his voice breaking.

"The day before Christmas Eve in 2018, the THP family went to my dad's place to sing carols. He was lying in bed and they came, instruments in tow, and sang for him before he was called home to the Lord on Christmas Eve."

It is not just the residents who become a part of THP family. Their families are brought into the fold as well. The THP family paid a special visit to Kelvin Choo's dad to sing Christmas carols to him in his final moments. Photo from The Hiding Place.

Ps Tan Hock Seng (*left*), together with Ps Philip (*right*), thanking God for helping THP to secure a permanent home. Photo from Ps Philip Chan's Facebook.

THE BLESSING

Tan Hock Seng's elder brother took him to THP in 1981, when he was just 23, in the hope that he would stop his drug habit.

Little did he know that he would go on to stay at THP for the next 39 years and counting. All because of an exchange he had overheard.

At the time, he had just joined THP's programme and, by his own admission, was no angel.

"Eh, how is Hock Seng?" he overheard his elder brother asking Ps Philip during a family visit.

"Don't worry, he's a blessing!" came Ps Philip's swift reply.

"I was thinking in my heart, 'I'm not a blessing *lah* … why he say like that?' I realised Ps Philip was saying that by faith. So that really stuck in my mind – to be a blessing," said Ps Hock Seng, 62, who now oversees the halfway house.

LEGACY OF LOVE

Sart S, a THP resident-turned-staff, also recounts the many times when residents hurled abuse at Ps Philip due to some misunderstanding and left the halfway house on a sour note.

"Sometimes after that, they would call, asking to return as they had gotten into trouble again," said Sart, 65, who oversees discipline in the home. "Ps Philip would tell us to take the boy in. Even when we reminded him of what happened in the past, he would say, 'Never mind *lah*, learn to love them. Just love them.'"

He recalled another time when he was interviewing a potential resident and his family. This was the family's third interview and they had asked to meet Ps Philip as he had not been present during the earlier interviews.

Sart asked for the family's understanding as Ps Philip had become increasingly ill and was resting after a medical appointment at the hospital.

The room where they met was just next to Ps Philip's bedroom. Upon overhearing the conversation, Ps Philip hobbled out to meet with the boy and his family.

Despite his tiredness, ill health and spinal issues that made walking painful, Ps Philip grabbed any chance he could to fulfil God's call on his life, which is also THP's mission:

We proclaim Him, admonishing every man and teaching every man with all wisdom, so that we may present every man complete in Christ. (Colossians 1:28-29)

The musician had been a resident at THP from 1991 to 2000 before leaving for an overseas music stint. While overseas, he started taking drugs again. "If there is one place that can help me turn my life around, it is The Hiding Place. So I called Ps Philip and he told me to come back immediately.

"I thank God for Ps Philip. The burden that God placed on his heart to love all of us has changed and touched so many lives, including mine and my family's. I will never forget the way he loved us and taught us to love others."

◆ Text by Geraldine Tan

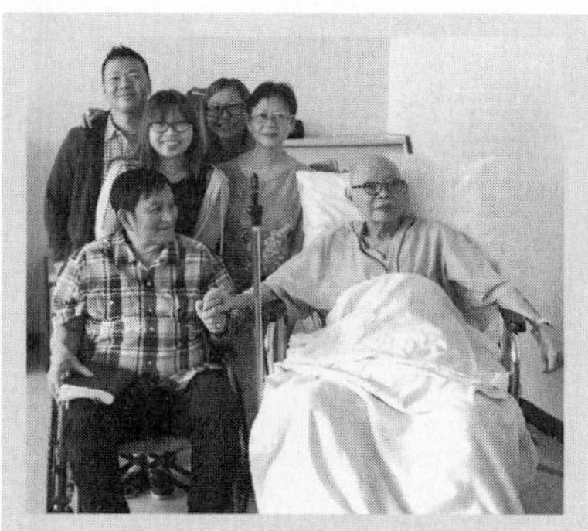

Despite his ill health towards the end of his life, Ps Philip never passed up on opportunity to minister to the THP boys and their families. He is pictured here with Kelvin's dad. Photo from Ps Philip Chan's Facebook.

Sart S (*middle, back row*), together with fellow THP staff Caleb Tan (*left*), Ps Philip (*right*) and Christina (*foreground*). Even though Sart failed to remain drug-free after leaving THP in 2000, Ps Philip welcomed him back in 2010. Ps Philip's love so touched Sart that he has stayed on as a staff of THP ever since. Photo from Ps Philip Chan's Facebook.

Editor's Note: Pastor Philip went home to the Lord in February 2020.

Faith

"If God doesn't heal, then what?": The heart-wrenching question that Pastor Philip Lyn had to grapple with

Ps-Dr Philip Lyn with his wife, Nancy (*right*), and Sarah (*middle*). All photos courtesy of Philip Lyn.

Strangled by a rope hanging from a clothesline, four-year-old Sarah Lyn was found clinically dead – her heart had stopped beating for more than five minutes.

A child's play that went awry.

When she was found, her face was dark blue and her pupils dilated. Sarah was somehow successfully resuscitated, but her contorted limbs indicated extensive brain damage.

It was August 26, 2002 – the day before her fourth birthday.

In the hospital, she lay in a coma for close to 12 hours – before God worked a miracle and healed her completely.

It was an unnatural, out-of-the-ordinary intervention by God.

Today, 16 years later, Sarah is a final-year medical student.

WAITING AND NOT KNOWING

While in the midst of despair, our perception of reality often challenges the truths of God – His goodness, His sovereignty and even His existence. God is sometimes even accused of being absent in and unaffected by our suffering and trials.

"If God doesn't heal my child, she's going to live with severe brain damage."

But this was not the case for Sarah's dad, Ps-Dr Philip Lyn, a medical doctor and bi-vocational pastor, and his wife, Nancy. Even though, in the 12 hours that passed between Sarah's accident and her full recovery, no one knew what would – or would not – happen.

The parents were in a liminal space – a place of transition, waiting, and not knowing.

The heaviness of those 12 hours, Dr Lyn and his wife would have felt it in the most acute ways.

Nevertheless, their faith in God's goodness and presence was sustained by the promise of the verse God reminded them of in Psalm which says: "I shall not die, but live, and declare the works of the LORD." (Psalm 118:17).

Dr Lyn recounted his thoughts then: "As a doctor, I was like, Okay, if God doesn't heal my child, she's going to live with severe brain damage and impairment.'

Sarah (*left*) and Dr Lyn (*righ*) at the Mt Kinabalu summit in 2014.

"I'd probably have to leave Kota Kinabalu and either move to Singapore or somewhere where my child can get better rehabilitation and special schooling."

His wife Nancy, on the other hand, was more emotional.

"She thought very much along the lines of the pain." Dr Lyn explained: "The pain that Sarah would have felt in her final moments before she blacked out.

> "We are going to serve the Lord. We are not going to back off."

"Nobody came. Sarah was probably thinking, 'Where's Mum? How come Mum's not here?'

"That was a severe source of pain to Nancy – the pain of not being there when Sarah needed her.

"Between the two of us – separately – we made a resolute decision before God. Whether Sarah would die or come out of this alive with permanent brain damage."

Dr Lyn paused before he continued: "We are going to serve the Lord. Continually. With all our hearts.

"We're not going to back off."

GOD CAN, GOD WILL

At the time of the accident, Dr Lyn was one year into pastoring a church and working as a medical doctor at the same time. The church was in its infancy then.

Having seen many miracles, Dr Lyn is no stranger to the un-natural work that God does. Yet, he says: "But when something so personal happens, it is *completely* different – spiritually, emotionally and mentally."

Dr Lyn said: "I think, the experience has grounded our faith.

"It has strengthened my conviction that God does heal and still does miracles today."

One important point that Dr Lyn is quick to emphasise, however, is the "even-if" aspect of his experience. He observed that, sometimes people see 'faith' as: God can. God will. And God *must*. But there needs to be a backstop to it: 'If God doesn't, then what?'

"Will we still have that same faith? Will you still believe in the God Who Is?"

"That's how our journey of faith has rounded off for us. The fullness of faith having a 'front' and 'back' to it."

"I preach a faith that God can and *God* will."

It is about seeing who God really is – and believing in Him.

But one thing Dr Lyn has learnt about faith is the personal aspect of it.

FAITH IS PERSONAL

He and Nancy were not the only witnesses to Sarah's miracle – his older children, Frances and Andrew, were there too.

"It doesn't matter how big – or how close – the miracle is, you need to experience God for *yourself*."

Frances was in her teenage years, while Andrew was in his pre-teens. Both of them had kept a prayer vigil alongside family and friends.

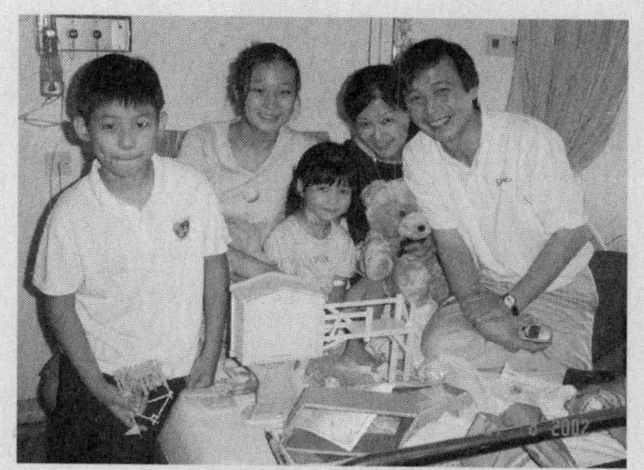

The Lyn family on August 27, 2002, in the hospital on Sarah's fourth birthday. She was discharged that same day, just one day after her accident.

Despite that, Dr Lyn recalls that they had the usual struggles and doubts about God – about His silence, His presence, and at times, even the reality of God.

"You would think to yourself, 'Your sister's been raised from the dead, for goodness sake!'

"When I talk to them about God being real, about how God speaks to them and about how close are you to God – they never refer to the miracle that happened to Sarah.

"They just didn't use it as a reference point for their faith. And it rarely ever came up."

He reckoned: "It doesn't matter how big – or how close – the miracle is, you need to experience God for *yourself*."

Even Sarah, herself, has had to own her faith journey – despite being the receiver of the miraculous healing.

Two to three months after the incident in 2002, the Lyns found that Sarah experienced no psychological scarring.

"We ventured to tell her about it," Dr Lyn recalled. "She was rather nonplussed, maybe a little surprised. It turns out that she has no memory of the event, it's what we call 'retrograde amnesia'."

"I had to seek Him for myself, and let God reveal Himself to me."

Sarah, who is now a 22-year-old, said: "When my parents first told me about the whole incident, I remember being confused as to why it was a big deal.

The Lyn siblings: (*from left*) Andrew, Sarah and Frances. All three siblings are committed disciples of Christ who are actively serving Him.

"I honestly thought that what had happened was a normal thing."

Then Sarah shared that, despite her realisation that what had happened was a miracle, "my faith journey was like anyone else's – full of ups and downs.

"I definitely questioned my faith multiple times. Sometimes, I took the 'devil's advocate' route and challenged my parents and other pastors on the nature of God, and the validity of the Bible. Other times I took the 'emotional' route, where I doubted God's presence because I couldn't feel Him."

Whichever route she took, Sarah soon found that she would never be satisfied with answers that were not her own. She said: "I had to seek Him for myself, and let God reveal Himself to me."

"It's incredibly strange," Dr Lyn said with a laugh. "They've experienced a great miracle but they still had to encounter God personally in their own inner life."

Faith is not built on miracles – or the lack of them. And every member of the Lyn family has had to reckon with the reality of God; be it in a commitment to serve Him or otherwise.

Today, Dr Lyn's church, Skyline SIB, is over a thousand-strong, and the couple is still serving faithfully alongside a team of other bi-vocational pastors. His children, Frances, Andrew and Sarah, are committed disciples of the Lord.

◆ **Text by Tan Huey Ying**

Faith

"I thought I was forgotten, but today I know that God knows me": A starving widow in Africa

In just a few months, God enabled Singaporean missionary to Africa, Jemima Ooi, and local leaders, to triple the number of people they were feeding as they weathered the effects of COVID-19. Ooi (*left*) is pictured here in a refugee settlement in Kenya with a village elder, a refugee woman and her pastor's wife. All photos courtesy of Jemima Ooi.

When Singaporean missionary Jemima Ooi, 32, heard in February that a coronavirus was sweeping across Asia and Europe, she knew it would only be a matter of time before it arrived in full force on Africa's shores.

And when it did arrive, anticipated Ooi, who works in war-afflicted refugee communities in Kenya, Congo and Rwanda, its impact on the people she had come to embrace as her own would be devastating.

"Sometimes we hear mothers wailing in despair because their child had died of hunger and didn't wake up that day."

Ooi worried not just about the region's inadequate healthcare capabilities, but also about the economic fallout from measures implemented to curb the spread of the virus.

If countries went into lockdown, her people – most of whom live hand to mouth – would not be able to work or eat, she thought. Furthermore, if borders closed, supply chains would crumble, driving up the cost of food.

It would be a fatal blow to these communities she has been working with for the past seven years, which includes shunned Ebola survivors, HIV patients, war refugees and massacre survivors.

Many of them are already so destitute that survival itself is a daily challenge, Ooi told *Salt&Light*.

Some can only afford to eat once every three days. Women, particularly those who have been abandoned by their husbands, are often driven to prostitution just to put food on the table for their children.

Even then, it is still not enough. "Sometimes we hear mothers wailing in despair because their child had died of hunger and didn't wake up that day," said Ooi.

"This is the reality we're in. With COVID-19 thrown into the equation and food becoming too expensive, you're thinking mass starvation."

DIVINE FORESIGHT

As Ooi and her team of local leaders in each field grappled with the impending fallout, they began to feel what Ooi calls a "Spirit-led urgency" to stock up on essential foods like rice, maize, flour, vegetables, beans, sugar and salt.

"We wanted to stockpile food so that when prices got too high, at least we would have a whole storehouse that we could give or

After food became too expensive, these young boys spent their mornings hunting grasshoppers to eat, said Ooi.

The Lord gave Ooi and her local leaders the foresight to stock up on food for their communities, such as rice, maize, grains, beans, vegetables, oil and charcoal, before food prices soared.

resell to our people at a price they can afford," said Ooi.

Their plan proved to be life-saving.

By March, the number of COVID-19 cases in African countries had begun to climb, prompting governments to shut their borders. As Ooi had feared, the price of food "skyrocketed".

A woman's daily wages, earned from labouring in the fields for 10 hours straight, were no longer enough to buy a 2kg bag of flour for her family. Families returned home from the market empty-handed and resigned to starvation.

In one area that Ooi works in, almost every household had children lying on the floor, so malnourished and weak with hunger and sickness that they could not even sit or stand up.

In another area, her team who visited one of the villages found families boiling grass to eat, she said.

But thanks to the divine foresight that the Lord had put in their hearts, Ooi and her teams were able to provide food from their stockpiles to more than 800 families by mid-March.

Upon receiving the food rations, one mother of five in a refugee settlement told a local leader: "I thought I was forgotten, but today I know that God knows me."

GOD KNEW WHAT WAS COMING

Looking back, Ooi, whose passion is to raise up and empower local leaders who care for their communities, marvels at how God had prepared her teams for the fallout of COVID-19.

In Kenya, local leaders had already started stockpiling food last year when the country suffered a prolonged season of drought and famine. During that time, they had also identified the most vulnerable families and set up mercy teams to take care of them.

Ooi (*second from right*) with her missionary buddy Liz (*left*) and two local leaders in Rwanda. Ooi's passion is to raise up and empower local leaders and missionaries to care for their own people.

This existing structure ensured that food could now be stockpiled effectively and distributed to those who needed it the most, said Ooi.

In Rwanda, the Lord had also prompted Ooi's team to buy a one-hectare banana plantation last year. She had thought of it as an investment, to sell it off later at a higher price and plough the money back into the ministry.

But the bananas and plantains turned out to be a food bank that has fed and sustained some 200 HIV-positive widows and their families during this period, said Ooi.

"God knew what was coming and He prepared us way in advance," she said.

FEED MY SHEEP

In March, the 800 families – or about 6,000 people – she and her teams were feeding had seemed like a lot, Ooi said, admitting that she had felt uncertain if they could keep it up.

"We don't know how long COVID-19 is going to last. We don't know how long we have to sustain them. We don't know if we will have the resources," she said.

But she heard the Lord speak to her clearly from Genesis 26:12. "Like Isaac, God wanted me to sow in a time of famine," said Ooi.

To her, this meant continuing to stockpile in faith, even though food prices were soaring. So, she liquidated projects that were

To cut costs, these local leaders from Kenya bought grain straight from farmers and wholesalers and processed the grain themselves before packing them into bags of 90kg for storage.

non-urgent and threw all the funds into increasing their food banks.

To circumvent the high prices, her teams went straight to farmers and wholesalers, and set up their own processing and packaging facilities.

Meanwhile, the needs of the people were increasing, with more families in need of rations.

Ooi said: "I remember taking a deep breath and thinking, 'Okay God, how are we going to do this? How are we going to continue?'"

As she mulled over these questions while out on a walk one night, she had an encounter with Jesus.

"I felt like He was standing right beside me," Ooi said. "And He said, 'Jem, don't hold back. If you love Me, feed My sheep, and do it well (John 21:15-17).'"

WALKING-ON-WATER EXPERIENCE

Both emboldened and humbled by this encounter, Ooi obeyed. "Okay God," she said to the Lord. "I will feed everyone whom You send my way."

As more needy families in each community were brought to their attention, Ooi and her teams took them under their wing and committed to providing for them.

A local leader (*extreme right*) found this family praying for food when he arrived with rations. The family's mother (*second from left*) is a widow who had to stop working after the factory she was working in was shut during the lockdown.

This Ugandan mother-of-four (*second from left*) was without a breadwinner as her husband was stranded in Kenya due to the lockdown. In a message from a pastor that Ooi works with, he said: "She testified that by the time I visited, they had nothing to eat and this was a divine provision."

Ooi also began receiving requests for help from pastors and missionaries outside of her fields, who were struggling to feed their communities. They shared that God had directed them to her.

"I was like, '*Wah,* God. You say one *ah!*'" said Ooi with a laugh. "I was really just standing in faith to see Him provide for all the people He wanted us to."

This widow (*right*), who has two children, took in another three kids when their parents were killed in an accident. On the day that leaders arrived with rations, she said that they were all prepared to go another night without any food. She exclaimed: "It's like living the Bible ... God is the God of widows and orphans!"

"I remembered feeling like we were under God's obsession for the poor and the broken."

And provide He did, as the Holy Spirit moved a group of people in Singapore to rise up and help.

"I never asked anyone for help, but miraculously, friends and family started giving generously and even thanked us for helping them sow into the lives of the severely impoverished.

"So stage by stage, we just faithfully provided and provided. And it was like the story of the widow and her small jar of oil in

2 Kings 4 – we poured the oil from the vase and realised it wasn't running out!" said Ooi in amazement.

"It's been a real walking-on-water experience of exercising faith. But in the midst of everything, I remembered feeling like we were under God's obsession for the poor and the broken.

"God is behind this. He's not going to let His people die."

The father (*right*) with a local leader after chancing upon the church's storehouse and being loaded up with provisions. Before this, he had walked fruitlessly for 30km in search of food for his hungry family.

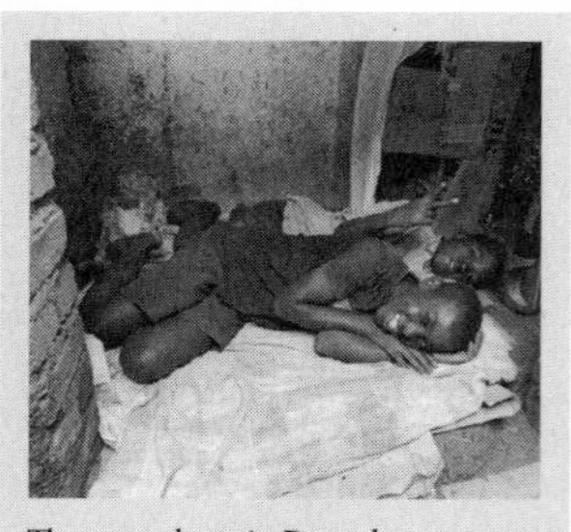

These two boys in Rwanda came to a storehouse begging for food one day. They had lost their parents to HIV and were living in a small mud-brick house that they had built themselves. "When they told the local leader their story, she cried, and they comforted her!" Ooi said.

GOD'S OBSESSION FOR THE POOR

By God's grace, Ooi and the local leaders were able to triple the number of families they were feeding. They are currently providing for almost 20,000 people, including many whom they believe God had sent to them.

In Uganda, where Ooi works with destitute communities, a man had gone out in search for food for his hungry family, only to come up short after walking for 30km. On his way home, he saw a sign for a church and turned into it, hoping someone in there would spare him just a cup of water.

Instead, he met the church's pastor and his wife, who generously loaded him up with sacks of food from their stockpile. The man could not help but cry with relief, said Ooi.

Over in Rwanda, two boys in ratty clothes had come to their storehouse begging and pleading for food. A local leader later found out that they were orphans whose parents had died from HIV. They were living alone in a self-built mud-brick house the size of a cabinet.

The leader cried after hearing their story, provided them with some food and put them on her radar so she could continue looking out for them.

Ooi said: "The amazing thing is that all this food distribution and building up of these Joseph storehouses have caused people who are so destitute to come out of the woodwork. We never knew they existed in our communities, but now we can bring them into our fold."

HOW MUCH FAITH?

As the number of COVID-19 cases in Africa rises – as of June 15, the continent has recorded more than 240,000 cases and 6,500 deaths – she and her teams are expecting to continue providing for many in the months to come.

But Ooi is convinced and assured that God is the One who ultimately provides.

While it is easy to feel inadequate when she looks at the overwhelming needs of the people around her, she has learnt to bring those feelings to the Lord and humbly ask what He would like her to do for Him.

"Once I gained God's heart for these people, I stopped being afraid of lack because I know that He is sending me to them and He has got the solutions.

"Really, the limiting factor is my mind. The limiting factor is my faith. I wondered, how many people can we feed?

"We can feed as many people as God wants us to. The real question is: How many do I have the faith to feed?"

◆ **Text by Gracia Lee**

HIV-positive widows in Rwanda receiving food rations for their families. During this time, many of them had taken the initiative to sew masks for their fellow villagers, said Ooi.

Faith

My name is Raymond and I am an ex-convict

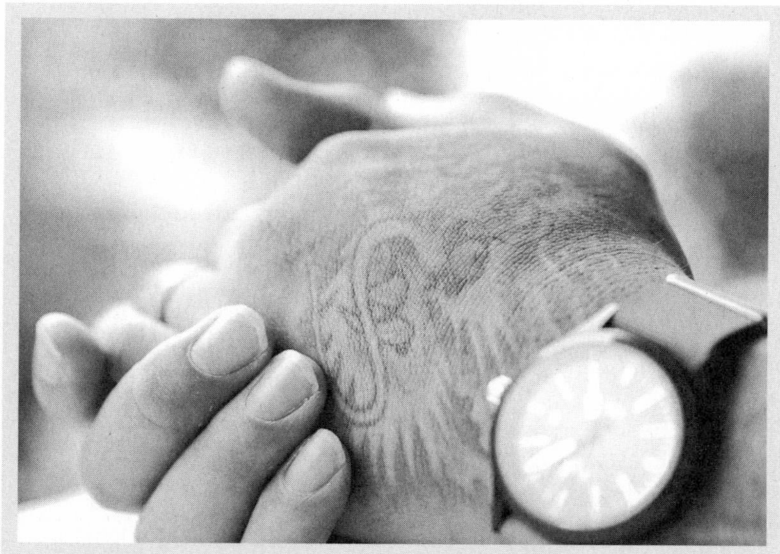

"God is real," says ex-convict Raymond Lim. "If you think you are not good enough to have a relationship with God, look at me. If Jesus died for someone as corrupt as I was, He would die for you too." Photo by David Lawrence Lim.

Redemption for ex-convict Raymond Tan began over a bowl of wanton noodles. Crab wanton noodles, to be exact. But the road to redemption had been a long and rocky one.

Raymond, 31, was born to a young woman with so many relationships that his surname was changed three times. His father abandoned the family when Raymond was just a baby. He never knew why.

His attractive, young mother worked long hours at DFS (duty free shop) and it was beyond his grandparents, with whom he lived, to properly supervise the bright but wayward boy.

"I was mischievous," recounted Raymond. "And one day my grandmother said to me, *'If I know you like that, I sell you away, don't take back already.'* "

It turned out that he had been sold to a Pasir Panjang vegetable seller when he was three months old. But was later taken back by his remorseful mother. His self-worth plummeted when he realised how unwanted he really was.

CRIME AND PUNISHMENT

At age 10, his life of crime began.

He stole $400 from his grandmother, who at the time was a successful insurance agent.

"From young, I felt that I had no worth. Money was the one thing that could give me worth," he said. He spent the money at an arcade.

His grandparents found out and retribution was swift.

"My grandfather was a dealer in amulets and idols," Raymond said. "Whenever I was caught stealing, he made me kneel in front of the idols for many hours. I was afraid – the idols looked scary and kneeling for so long was unbearable. I hated it."

Yet punishment did not deter Raymond from further criminal activity.

At 12, he was caught stealing fishing tackle from NTUC supermarket. But a kind man came to his rescue.

"He told the supermarket manager, 'This kid made a mistake' and he paid for me," Raymond recalled. "Sometimes we think we are doing good, but we might not be. When the man paid my bill, I escaped punishment and didn't learn my lesson. I remember thinking it was easy to get away with crime.

"So I got bolder. I stole more at home and outside. I even instigated my friends to steal packets of *nasi lemak* from a food stall, and we sold them to nearby pedestrians."

TEENAGED MASTERMIND

"I was often the mastermind, so the other kids looked up to me. All of us came from broken families and we stayed out late at night.

"We shook out vending machine coins, broke into bus yards and stole money, CD players and LCD TVs from the buses.

One judge said to me: "Save your crocodile tears. You are not just an offender. You have a criminal mind."

"We bought the latest handphones, bicycles, hung out at billiard bars, drank, smoked."

Things came to a head when 12-year-old Raymond was caught stealing at Takashimaya. The crime fell into the category of "theft in dwelling" and he was put in a pre-court guidance programme.

"The counsellors in the guidance programme were big-hearted. But it was very difficult to make a change if the youth had other bad influences in his or her life," said Raymond matter-of-factly.

By 16, he was hanging out in the back streets of Geylang, where he and his friends conducted illegal gambling activities. They sold fake cough mixture in bulk to addicts, mixing in Coca Cola and sugar to bulk up the volume. He heard that other people even added kerosene.

He was caught when he broke into a house to steal liquor, and was remanded in Boys' Home for almost two years. But he was undeterred.

During national service, he got into credit card fraud and was thrown in prison. Just 21 days after his release, he was caught stealing on a cruise ship. By that time he had been in Boys' Home and prison five times.

"One judge said to me, 'Save your crocodile tears. You are not just an offender. You have a criminal mind.'

"Thankfully, I had never been sentenced to more than a year, whereas if you are sentenced to Corrective Training (CT), it is a minimum of five years."

This time, CT seemed inescapable. But, miraculously, he was sentenced to just 30 days. Deep down he knew God was at work.

But the life of crime proved too enticing. He fraudulently got a bank loan to acquire six cars and started a car rental business, parking his cars at Pasir Ris Park and advertising his services online.

Eventually his fleet grew to over 30 cars and he became a millionaire at the age of 24.

IN LOVE

At 23, Raymond discovered he was to be a father. His then girlfriend, Vivian, had stuck with him through thick and thin. ("As in, she knew me when I was thin, and now she's still with me when I'm thick," he chuckled.)

They had met in secondary school. She was an express student and they bumped into each other during the school fire drill.

"I pestered her friend to ask her to go out with me until she said yes," Raymond said with a laugh.

"I looked in my wallet: $40. The milk powder was $69. I didn't even have enough money to buy milk for my baby."

"Her parents, the school, her friends ... everyone told her that there would be no good outcome to our relationship. Yet she stuck with me. I didn't even appreciate her except when I was in prison. Whenever I was released, I would return to the company of my friends.

"I was not thinking of marriage. But when I heard she was pregnant, we decided to marry. Coming from a broken childhood, I did not want my child to grow up unwanted like me."

They lived the high life, driving posh cars and living in a condominium, as Raymond's business was doing well. When he bought 4D, he would drop $40,000 to $60,000 at a time. ("That's how much of a gambler I was.")

But he was living like a single man, gambling all day and hanging out with his friends all night. Inevitably the marriage fell apart and the two were estranged.

"I squandered all my money at the casino. At my condo balcony I prayed, 'God, the only way for me to get back my money is to gamble more. Please help me win.'

"That day I went to the casino and ... I never lost money so fast in my life! Before long, I had almost nothing left. It was as though Jesus was telling me: *It's time. You need to hit rock bottom before you rise again*.

"I went home and my intention was to commit suicide. But then my wife told me that she was pregnant again. And I couldn't jump. I couldn't do that to my children. So we decided to reconcile.

"The next day I went to buy milk powder and I looked in my wallet: $40. The milk powder was $69. I didn't even have enough money to buy milk powder for my baby."

That was rock bottom. And that was when Raymond, recalling his own bleak childhood and not wishing the same upon his children, decided to pick himself up.

ROCK BOTTOM

He decided to start a crab wanton noodle stall in Macpherson.

Despite working hard day and night, business was not good. He emailed well-known food bloggers, but none replied except one – Dr Leslie Tay of ieatishootipost fame.

Unknown to Raymond, when Dr Tay, a Christian, received his email, he felt a strong prompting to help this particular hawker.

The next day, Dr Tay and his wife appeared unannounced at Raymond's stall. He gave Raymond a few pointers and then noticed the cross around his neck.

"You a Christian?" Dr Tay asked.

"*Er* ... I don't know. I think so?" said Raymond.

"But you don't go to church?"

"No."

Dr Tay invited Raymond to his Anglican church, St John's-St Margaret's.

"I thought, 'If I don't go to church, he might not help me'," said Raymond. "So I went to church ... but for the wrong reasons!"

It was Easter, and during the hymns, "tears kept flowing and I kept cleaning them away. I asked the doctor, 'What is happening?' and he said, 'You are touched by the Lord.' When the altar call came, I went up and said the Sinner's Prayer.

"The next day I was at my hawker stall. At the end of the day, it was my habit to light a cigarette in the back alley.

"I was still thinking of the previous day's experience in church, and I looked up at the sky and said, 'God, if you are real, help me to stop smoking ... But please don't take too long, otherwise I will think it is my own will power and not you!'

"The next morning, I lit up a cigarette as was my custom. *Wah, why the cigarette taste like that?* I went down to the shopkeeper and said, 'Did you change your supplier? Your cigarette tastes bad!' He said, 'No.'

"I was in a rush to open up my stall, so I went off. During my break, I went to the back alley with a new box of cigarettes. Before I could light one, I smelt the smoke from all the smokers around me and ... I gagged.

"I had been smoking since I was 12 years old and had tried to quit many times but the smoke had been too alluring to me. Yet now I was gagging! That was when I knew for sure that God is real."

THE VINE AND THE VINEDRESSER

That was one-and-a-half years ago. Raymond's life took an about turn. His marriage strengthened and he lost the desire to gamble.

"God really is the vinedresser," said Raymond. "It was as if He was trimming away everything in my life that was not fruitful. God amazes me every day."

> "I was trapped in my gambling addiction to the extent that I hurt all the people closest to me."

A Filipina Christian who prayed and prophesied over his wife, told her: "Those days when you cried under your blanket and asked God if He was real? God wants you to know that He heard you."

He prayed for a change of jobs because of the long hours, and soon after, his ex-staff dropped by Raymond's stall. He was astounded by the change he saw in Raymond – "I used to be hot tempered and vulgar" – and offered him a partnership in a vehicle recovery business.

The manageable working hours allows Raymond to volunteer at the Boys' Home. Where once he was a resident delinquent, he is now their mentor. The boys see his tattoos and know immediately that this is a man who has walked in their shoes.

"At one point, I was trapped in my gambling addiction to the extent that I hurt all the people who loved me and were closest to me," said Raymond. "Blinded by greed, I lied, I stole, I cheated. The ones who cared deeply for me were the ones I hurt the most. In desperation, I stole from friends, lied to my in-laws so that they lent me their life savings, and cheated my grandparents into selling their house and giving me a big part of the sale.

"Looking back, I really felt I deserved hell … until God showed me His love, His mercy, His grace. The day I received God's forgiveness was when I truly understood what it meant when Jesus said in the Gospels that he who has been forgiven much, loves much. Luke 7:41-43

"God reached out to me so many times, but human beings have a short memory," he said sheepishly. "When you get what you want, you forget about God. But God never forgot about me."

His flat in Bedok Reservoir is a haven of peace, with Bible verses – Ephesians 2:1-5, Psalm 91:4, Psalm 23:1-6 – painted on every sky blue wall.

"I want my family to be reminded of the presence of God everywhere we turn," said Raymond, who attends Bible study with a men's group on Thursdays and church with his wife Vivian, two-year-old son Vernon, and five-year-old daughter Vera, on Sundays.

"God is real," he emphasised. "If you think you are not good enough to have a relationship with God, look at me. If Jesus died for someone as corrupt as I was, He would die for you too."

◆ **Text by Juleen Shaw**

"How do I lead by loving others?" Claire Wong, Head of DBS Foundation, on the key principle in her leadership

"When I look at my life today, I don't think I could have imagined that this is what it would look like," said Claire Wong, Head of DBS Foundation. Photo by Glen Goh.

Claire Wong helms the DBS Foundation, championing social entrepreneurship in Asia. In 2019, the Foundation was the inaugural winner of the Social Enterprise Champion (Corporation) award. The recognition from the President's Office honours business organisations' contribution to the local social enterprise sector.

Salt&Light sat down with 44-year old Claire Wong to talk about her faith that keeps her anchored as a business leader in the marketplace and, at home, as wife and mother.

As a product of Sunday school, Wong knew the Lord as a child. At 19, with an Economic Development Board (EDB) scholarship to the London School of Economics tucked under her belt, she was pursuing the Singapore Dream but not quite God's plan for her life. She relates to *Salt&Light* how getting on board with God's agenda changed the way she now lives every aspect of her life:

WAS THERE A TURNING POINT IN YOUR LIFE?

I was a typical Singaporean student, definitely very driven by results.

"Many of these caring moments can become Gospel moments."

At university, I saw many friends become Christians and, their lives were changed but I didn't see that same change in my own life. I was still pursuing the same things as before – the perfect grades and a good career. I questioned if I was really a Christian.

The final year of my master's degree (MPhil, Economics, University of Cambridge) was very difficult. My course-mates were either having mental breakdowns or were so driven by the need to pursue the course. It made me think if chasing that piece of paper was really that important.

God used that to help me see that, if I was really a Christian, then there should be some change in my life priorities. Getting good grades should not be the only, and topmost, thing in my life.

God challenged me: If I truly believed in Jesus and wanted to follow Him, He had to be the Lord over my life and in my decisions and priorities. I needed to trust Him, not in myself.

That was a turning point in my life.

Claire (*third from right*) and the DBS Foundation team together with President Halimah Yacob. Picture courtesy of Claire Wong.

HOW DO YOU BRING GOD'S PURPOSE TO WORK?

Christians sometimes struggle with their purpose at work, it's like: "I'm just going to get this (the work) over and then I'm off to church for Bible studies at night." But I think the nine hours you spend at work is just as important.

I tell myself, I'm a disciple of Christ – at home with my kids, at work and at church. I try to use all the opportunities God has given.

I am a Christian at the workplace as much as I'm a Christian in church. It is about being faithful, bringing God's glory in everything, seeing myself as an ambassador of Christ.

God doesn't compartmentalise our lives – having that mindset changes the way you work.

The key principle in every decision is to consider: How do I love others? How do I lead? Does this please God, does it glorify Him? How do I reflect the Gospel? And then looking for opportunities to share.

So before I send the email, especially when I'm angry about something, and want to say "something", I ask myself: "Would people be led closer to God or will they be stumbled by what I say?"

It's the motivation, that broader perspective, just thinking about pleasing God as your Master in everything that you do, that makes the difference.

HOW DO YOU SEEK OPPORTUNITIES TO SHARE AT WORK?

Opportunities come in many forms and could be random.

There was this colleague in my workplace I didn't really know. Someone had told me that there was a tragedy in her family. So when I bumped into her in the toilet, I said: "I heard about this, am very sorry to hear that. If you would love to chat, we can have lunch."

It was amazing because we did have lunch and I realised another Christian had also reached out and shared the Gospel with her. She wasn't a believer then. So when I came along, I was the next person.

Some of the deepest friendships that I have developed at work come just from reaching out to someone. Many of these caring moments can become Gospel moments.

GOD'S WISDOM IN SECULAR WORK – IS THAT POSSIBLE?

The many decisions at work actually allow us to really seek His wisdom.

"Work situations bring about different things that God uses for our sanctification."

James 3:17-18 talks about wisdom from above. Godly wisdom is about the pursuit of righteousness. It's about loving others, showing care and concern.

Those verses struck me. It reminds me that this is the kind of wisdom that I want in my work decisions.

The workplace can be very harsh where showing compassion and love are almost alien.

The worldly wisdom is about who wins the argument or deal, even when they are done in the most un-peaceful and unrighteous way. Never mind that, you still won. So, I ask myself: Is that the battle I am fighting?

If you strive to please God, you would leave the things that are not in your hands to Him and, if someone's upset about it, I'd pray that God will take care of that.

Work situations bring about different things that God uses for our sanctification.

HOW DO YOU STEER CLEAR OF MATERIAL TRAPPINGS?

Material success and education are probably two big idols in our society.

That's not to say that I don't struggle with them, but when you're aware of them, you're more prepared to fight them. While the idols are desirable, I am conscious of the sinfulness that can come.

To live differently, you need to be counter-cultural. The idols in this society are so clear, so it is also very clear when you live counter-culturally, not chasing after the same things.

Claire with her husband, Eugene Low on holiday. The couple spent eight years in the United States. Picture courtesy of Claire Wong.

But being counter-cultural is a very powerful witness of the Gospel.

(To be counter-cultural, was something Claire faced eight years ago, when her husband, Eugene Low, decided to become a pastor. Reverend Eugene Low pastors at Grace Baptist Church. He was formerly the Washington Correspondent for *The Straits Times*.)

WHAT WERE YOUR THOUGHTS WHEN YOUR HUSBAND WENT INTO FULL-TIME MINISTRY?

To be honest, I was hoping that maybe God would change his mind! But being honest as well, I wrote out the list of fears I had – the fear of financial insecurity, fears that we wouldn't be able to provide for our children and have the life I had dreamed of.

"Being counter-cultural is a powerful witness of the Gospel."

It is about making an impact on society, which is really exciting," Claire Wong shares about her work at DBS Foundation. Picture by Glen Goh.

I spoke with Eugene and other Christian friends about my list. I went back to the Scriptures, challenging myself, wrestling with and allowing God to change my heart. And He did.

I realised that the list of things I struggled with about my husband's change in vocation were also idols in my heart. God was saying to me then: "Why do you not trust that I will provide?"

The struggle was much about me and God. It was part of my discipleship as a Christian, my cost of following Jesus and not what I'm giving up for my husband.

Throughout the period, I knew that it was where God was leading us to. I just needed to figure out how I could get there, how my heart could be aligned with God's heart, to desire what He desires.

HOW DID YOU NAVIGATE CHANGES IN YOUR CAREER?

On the first of January each year, my husband and I would sit down to talk about our life and priorities, which include work, church, kids, marriage.

"My job decisions have always been made with my husband."

It was in those general check-ins when I would feel God place change in my heart. We prayed about it, talked it out, sought counsel from people and waited to see where God was leading.

I'm thankful that, as a couple, we take time to talk about my career transitions, what they mean for us as a family, how my husband views it, supports and encourages me. In a way, my job decisions have always been made together, because Eugene also knows that he has to step up when I'm busy.

The transitions were not easy and the learning curves were steep. But in that time of change I also learned a lot about myself and my faith. I realised that there was still fear of man, and again, that achievement orientation – I really wanted to do well.

I had to turn to God and rely on Him. He helped me to see clearly and to persevere. The verse in Isaiah 41:10 was especially an encouragement during that season. It says: "Fear not, for I am with you; be not dismayed, for I am your God; I will strengthen you, I will help you, I will uphold you with my righteous right hand."

AS A WORKING MUM, HAVE YOU FELT ABSENT FROM YOUR KIDS' LIVES?

At times I do. It's really important to always evaluate and re-evaluate. It is also a question of how the kids are doing. Do they feel insecure, or have developmental issues and challenges as a result of your not being there?

It's about being willing to be honest about where things are and submitting to God. As Singaporeans, we hold on to our careers too tightly, such that if God is calling for a change, you are unable or unwilling. I'm not saying it's easy.

Actually I have been in that season. Eugene had just moved to a different church, I just had my second child and was in a consulting job. I felt things were not in order and I was unable to manage our home.

> "I do strongly believe that, if God has made you the mother of your children, only you can carry out the role."

I had to stop and evaluate. It was very hard. I stopped work and didn't have a timeline to it.

Managing your household has to be a priority, and when you say it's a priority, then you have to figure out how to make it a priority.

As a woman, especially in Singapore, I am aware that I should not outsource the role of being a mother or wife, because I do

"It's not just being physically present with the kids. It's also about being spiritually present with them," Claire Wong says of her parental responsibility. Her sons will turn 11 and 8 this year. Photo courtesy of Claire Wong.

strongly believe that God has made you the mother of your children and only you can carry out the role.

No one else, not the grandparent, not a helper can.

◆Text by Karen Tan

Mr Lee Kuan Yew and his CYC shirt: "God moments" in the journey of an iconic Singapore brand

Third generation scion of CYC, Fong Loo Fern (*left*), with longtime CYC tailor, Roland Tan (*right*), pictured here with Mr Lee Kuan Yew at the Istana in 2010, when they updated the founding Prime Minister's shirt measurements. All photos courtesy of Fong Loo Fern and CYC.

Nineteen years ago in 2001, a polka dotted shirt that was sentimental to Singapore's founding Prime Minister Lee Kuan Yew gave a leg up to then-flailing family business, CYC Shanghai Shirt Company.

Some 10 years ago, CYC's managing director Fong Loo Fern escaped without a scratch in an ATV (all-terrain vehicle) accident.

Most recently on April 3, 2020, Prime Minister Lee Hsien Loong's announcement encouraging the use of reusable masks could not have come at a more perfect time for the heritage tailoring brand known for their exacting Shanghainese craftsmanship. Their business had dipped by 80% when COVID-19 struck. But sales that weekend of their just-launched reusable cloth masks – a product of Fong's foresight – was beyond expectation.

The brand's call for the nation to help sew 300,000 masks for migrant workers received overwhelming support and also went viral across social media and the press.

"A lot of times, I ask for the Holy Spirit to please give me ideas."

Were these all coincidences?

In an interview with *Salt&Light*, Fong (née Chiang), 66, dismissed suggestions that these were a result of either coincidence or good business timing.

They were "God moments", she said.

"Who else would be able to engineer something like that but God?" said Fong, who is also the Chairman of Methodist Welfare Services.

(*Left to Right*) Loo Fern's father Chiang Sing Choo, uncle Chiang Ping Choo, grandmother Foo Ah Neok and grandfather Chiang Yick Ching.

Loo Fern at age 12, with her grandmother, Foo Ah Neok.

Fong has been blessed by many "God moments" in her life and in the business her grandparents, Chiang Yick Ching and Foo Ah Neok, founded 85 years ago when they came to Singapore from China in 1935 in search of a better life.

As the eldest grandchild, Fong was immersed in the family business from the tender age of 12, working as a cashier during school holidays.

She joined the company in 1977 after graduating from the National University of Singapore with a degree in accountancy.

Fong's proposal to update the merchandise and layout of the shops was rejected by her uncle and father who helmed the company. She left the family business in 1985.

The family business floundered in the rapidly-changing retail and economic climate of the 1970s and 1980s.

The brand was looking old-fashioned next to competition from newer, more contemporary brands and cheaper imports. Frequent warehouse sales to clear unsold stock hurt their image. Add to the mix a recession and an exit tax on Indonesian tourists who made up a significant portion of their clientele.

A SINKING SHIP

In 1992, Fong's uncle passed away from a heart attack. Two months later, her father suffered a severe stroke and was unable to continue working.

"Business was in deep trouble, like a ship with a lot of holes," said Fong.

She left her job with the US Embassy's Department of Commerce to steer the ship with her mum's help.

"I didn't have to spend money on renovations for a brand name location ... So, wow, that was a God moment."

"When I took over, I had to do a lot of painful things like restructure and sell off some assets." This included selling off their factory at MacPherson.

"Then I was left with two shops – in Circular Road and Tanglin Shopping Centre, an old shopping mall. The locations were not that great. The main shop at North Bridge Road was acquired by the government."

Fong hired consultants to help chart the long-term survival of the brand and revamp its image. She closed the division that produced ready-made shirts to focus on CYC's original roots: Bespoke shirts. (Besides their made to measure shirts, CYC today makes ready-to-wear shirts when orders are placed so that they don't stockpile inventory).

She set up a business arm to manufacture uniforms for corporate clients, which would contribute almost half of its turnover in 2002.

BRAND-NAME LOCATION

About two years after taking over the business, Fong was at the Tanglin Shopping Centre shop when she met long-time customer Richard Helfer, then General Manager of Raffles Hotel.

"He said, 'Hey, you really should come to Raffles Hotel. Because with your heritage, you should position yourself at one of the shops there.

"Business was so bad, how could we be at Raffles Hotel, such a high-end location, I thought."

CYC stores across the years (*from left*) Selegie Road, Raffles Hotel shopping arcade and Capitol Piazza.

Fong went to see a space that a tenant was giving up. It happened to be a menswear shop.

"I didn't have to spend money on renovations, and I was getting a brand-name location. So that was wow, a God moment to have that," says Fong. CYC would be at Raffles for 23 years until 2017.

"But it doesn't mean that you have a nice location, business will be good. We were still trying to reinstate our brand's heritage. We had a lot of old customers who continued to buy from us, but business was really tough."

THAT FAMOUS 36-YEAR-OLD SHIRT

Then in 2001, Fong ran a promotion with *The Business Times* to encourage customers to bring in their CYC shirts, with the view of building a collection of vintage shirts to exhibit.

"We had many customers at that time who told us, 'I've been a customer for 20 years', 'I've been a customer for 30 years'."

As an incentive, CYC gave a 20% discount to those who had shirts that were more than 10 years old, and a 50% discount for those who brought in shirts which were more than 20 years old. They gave a free shirt to customers who brought in shirts which were more than 30 years old.

> "That was really a God moment because no one could have engineered a PR story like that."

Mrs Lee Kuan Yew brought in three shirts that belonged to her husband, Singapore's founding Prime Minister.

"They had been our customers for a long, long time. Mrs Lee would come to our shops to place the orders for her husband. She was very simple, never asking for much.

"She told me that one of those shirts was sentimental to her and Mr Lee because he had worn that shirt during one of the rallies in 1965, 36 years ago.

"I thought it sounded like an amazing story that someone would keep a shirt for so long, especially Mr Lee Kuan Yew. I asked if I could share that story with the media.

"Mrs Lee said, 'Write something and I will ask Mr Lee for his permission.'

"So I sent in a short story to her. And, to my surprise, Mr Lee said that we could go ahead.

"So I sent the story to the press, thinking that no one would be interested. But everyone got so excited, and I got so much publicity from *The Straits Times*, *The Business Times*, even TV and the Chinese newspapers.

"That was really a God moment because no one could have engineered a PR story like that."

That God moment "brought a lot more awareness about what who we are and the work we do. And that helped create more awareness with the younger customers at that time".

Business picked up. The company outgrew their current store two years later, and moved to a bigger, more prominent space right next to the entrance of the shopping arcade at Raffles Hotel.

When the landmark hotel announced it was closing for an extensive makeover in 2017, Fong wondered how to relocate in the brief six months that tenants were given to move out.

Then someone told her about availability at Capitol Piazza. At that time, it was a small space meant for a pop-up. But two years later, the mall management took back the area as they were repurposing the second floor into a co-working space.

"We were given a larger ground floor unit at a very good rate – another blessing," Fong said.

The shirt that Mr Lee Kuan Yew wore at a 1965 rally was exhibited in 2002 along with other vintage CYC shirts at Raffles Hotel. All of Mr Lee's shirts had a tag of his name sewn in them, a spillover from his days as a student in England.

A SECRET CHRISTIAN

Fong came to the faith secretly when she was in Secondary Two.

Loo Fern as a child, with her mother Chan May Lee. Loo Fern's mother passed away at the end of July, at age 88.

"My grandmother was very anti-Christian. But the right thing she did was to send me to Methodist Girls' School (MGS). And so, I was brought up in a Christian school with Bible studies."

(Fong's grandmother, "a very strong autocratic person" took over the reins of the family business when her husband died in the 1949. "She had no choice. She had two sons to feed," said Fong. These two sons would eventually join the family business.)

Fong was inspired by the passion of her maths teacher, a Miss Wong, and "peer influence".

"Many of my friends at MGS were Christians. I was very sad that I couldn't go to church and join them in their activities. I fought with my grandmother and even my mum about going to church, because I wanted to be with my friends. You know how teenagers are – you want to do what your friends are doing.

"My grandmother was very anti-Christian.
But the right thing she did was
to send me to Methodist Girls' School."

"I wouldn't say that I was an active Christian at that time. But accepting Christ gave me peace," says Fong, referring to conflicts, sensitivities, work and other issues related to the family business.

Fong was not allowed to attend church, but she managed to push for a church wedding when she married into a Christian family.

The matriarch of the Chiang family saw her children becoming Christians. "I think that worried her because she was probably afraid that when she passed on, no one would pay respects to her in the temple."

Fong's grandmother passed on suddenly from a heart attack one night before the family had an opportunity to witness to her.

Fong's mother subsequently came to the faith when she accompanied Fong on a mission trip "where she saw that miracles are real". She went on to become "an avid mission trooper".

BAPTISM WITH THUNDER

Fong was baptised when she got married, but when a friend, a "*gung-ho*, enthusiastic Christian", asked if she had been baptised, Fong replied that she did not think she had been baptised by the Holy Spirit.

"It was really angels who protected me. I recall falling gently to the ground."

So they arranged to meet at the former golf driving range where Gardens by the Bay now stands. It was a weekday lunchtime some 15 years ago. The driving range was empty. The two friends were the only ones there.

"It was a nice quiet place. My friend began to pray for me. And suddenly, it started to rain. My eyes were closed. There was a thunderstorm and I heard the trees *whishing* by me. And I thought I heard footsteps. Then because I was very self-conscious, I opened my eyes and said, 'Okay, I think I've been baptised by the Holy Spirit.'"

Afterwards, the thought of the sound of the strong wind rustling the leaves niggled at Fong. "So one day, I decided to drive to the driving range. I saw that there were no trees nearby. The trees were so far away. How could I hear them so strongly? Oh my goodness, the Holy Spirit had been there.

"I felt that was the confirmation that I had the Holy Spirit in me."

ATV ACCIDENT

Nine years ago, during a family holiday at an island off Phuket, Fong experienced divine protection.

Loo Fern before the ATV accident. "It was really angels who protected me," she said of escaping without a scratch when the vehicle toppled over.

They had hired ATVs to ride.

"We were taught how to manage the vehicles at the resort, where there was very smooth ground. Then the guide took us single file out through jungle. The terrain became uneven and stony.

"There were a couple of rocks in front of me. And I was trying to avoid them. Instead of pressing the brakes, I pressed the accelerator. The bike went up a slope to my right, and I was thrown off the bike. The bike fell over. But it didn't fall on me. It fell to the left of me.

"My kids came to hold me up. 'Mum are you okay?' they asked.

"I felt myself. No scratch, no bruise, no broken back, no broken bones. This was amazing – I was over 50 years old, and to walk away from an accident like this …

"It was really angels who protected me. I recall falling gently to the ground.

"It's like God's protection, His favour. Sometimes I think I don't deserve this," said Fong, wiping tears from her eyes.

"Now that you made me think about this, you made me cry," she told *Salt&Light*, adding that God is so real in her life.

PRUDENCE AND WITTY INVENTIONS

About five years ago, Fong received the prophecy: "I wisdom dwell with prudence, and find out knowledge of witty inventions." (Proverbs 8:12, KJV). She keeps the verse "in my hands, on my mind".

"A lot of times, I ask for the Holy Spirit to please give me ideas. And it's really amazing how He give me ideas.

Apart from the reusable masks, other "witty inventions" that have come out of this age of COVID-19 have included the recently launched Work From Home Collection. It is the answer to the biggest challenge of work from home: Keeping cool in the humid weather "because you can't keep the air-con on 24/7", and looking good in Zoom meetings.

CYC is also looking at technology that would enable customers to customise their designs, or eventually take their own measurements.

As a Christian entrepreneur in a secular world, Fong says: "It's more challenging because everybody knows that we are Christian. You have to walk the talk. Otherwise you won't be a good reflection of Christ."

It's hard, says Fong who admits that she's "trying to downplay my domineering personality" while being sensitive to managing people. "I think it's all about striking a balance. Because if you say yes to everything, you won't get anything done. But if you bulldoze your way through things, you'll end up with a lot of hurt feelings.

"We really need prudence and courage in managing the different aspects of our business."

"Many times, I lose my temper or say the wrong things.

"Like I teach my grandkids, the most important word to say is 'sorry'. It's one of the most difficult words to say."

As a business person, she tries to espouse the four virtues set out in a Christian book on entrepreneurship, *Bringing your Business to Life*, by Jeffrey Cornwall and Michael Naughton.

"We really need prudence in managing the different aspects of our business. And then sometimes when we make decisions, we need to have courage to make that decision."

The other two virtues are justice and temperance.

One of her favourite Bible verses is Philippians 4:6-7: "Do not be anxious about anything, but in every situation, by prayer and petition, with thanksgiving, present your requests to God. And the peace of God, which transcends all understanding, will guard your hearts and your minds in Christ Jesus."

◆ **Text by Gemma Koh**

Work

My two copper coins: A doctor returns to the frontlines

"As Jesus looked up, he saw the rich putting their gifts into the temple treasury. He also saw a poor widow put in two very small copper coins. "Truly I tell you," he said, "this poor widow has put in more than all the others. All these people gave their gifts out of their wealth; but she out of her poverty put in all she had to live on." (Luke 21:1-4)

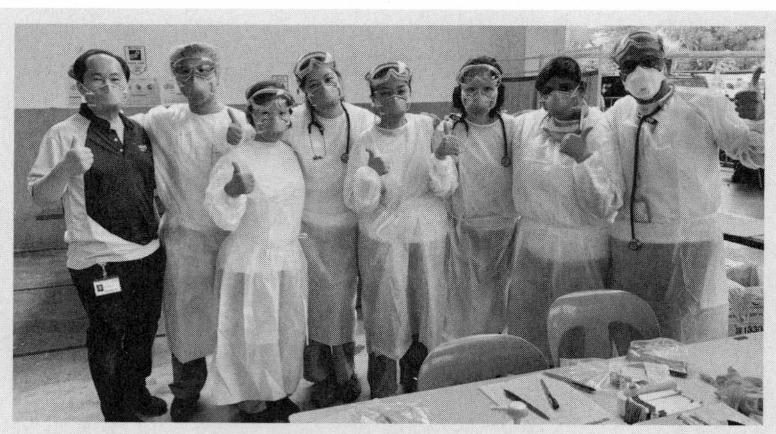

The medical team at a migrant dormitory led by Wai Jia's mentor, Prof Malcolm Mahadevan (*extreme right*), who led her back into clinical medicine. All photos courtesy of Dr Tam Wai Jia.

After seven years away from clinical work, it felt surreal that my first foray back to clinical work was into the thick of action, in full-blown personal protective equipment at a migrant dormitory.

A kind nurse taught me as I fumbled: "No, not like this, but like that."

I wore my gloves then touched a table. ("Aww shucks, you gotta change 'em, Doctor.") I degloved then regloved clumsily.

I asked silly questions: "So this is the triage right?"

It has been seven years since I saw my last patient in a hospital setting, before I went on to do public health and medical education.

Then, in the midst of my teaching medical students, I suffered a health complication requiring urgent surgery.

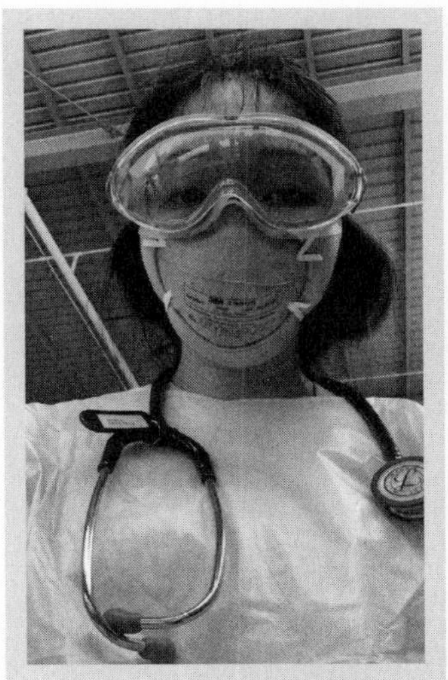

Masked, gowned and goggled for duty.

As I recovered in the luxury of my own home, it was as if time had stopped. And the pain of watching a pandemic play out while I could do nothing snapped something deep inside.

The day before Good Friday, I started to weep. And it would not stop.

I knew, after all these years, God was calling me back to the frontline.

BROKEN VESSELS

Tears. Fear. Questions.

Tears. How they ran down. The same recurrent memory of being shouted at as a junior doctor still strikes coldness in my heart. ("You stupid, stupid house officer!")

The hysterical crying that erupted when I broke bad news of a patient's unexpected death still haunts me.

"While the world champions vessels of might and power, God looks for broken ones, eager to be refashioned."

Fear. My husband, Cliff, is immunocompromised from his liver cancer and transplant. My two children are three and under.

Questions. How? When? Was I even capable of seeing patients anymore? Could I be useful? Wouldn't I be a burden?

For years I had suppressed traumatic incidents that had happened in my early years of clinical work. I believed I had unintentionally contributed to a patient's death, only hours after I had held her hand to assure her she would be discharged soon.

My seniors assured me that what had ensued was unforeseen. But I never quite recovered. I found comfort in the boundaries of public health and medical education, where I believed it was impossible to cause clinical harm.

Yet, in the furrows of an unfolding national disaster, I found myself weeping, pleading to God for answers.

How could I help? Even if I offered, who would want my skills?

For all my fancy accolades related to public health, I felt useless in this national crisis.

In desperation, I prayed for God to use me in some small way. Then, a more audacious prayer: God, bring me to the dormitories to help the migrant workers.

"It's impossible to go in – they're locked down," I was told.

Then, a miracle.

BETTER STILL

My mentor was tasked to lead a team to recce a dormitory. The same day, I was connected to a migrant health non-profit regarding creating mental health support for quarantined migrant workers.

As God led me, I connected the two organisations. The ground-up efforts of the migrant non-profit and the medical structure of a healthcare institution combusted into a collaboration to provide help to those who needed it most.

"Like the widow with two mites was I with my meagre offering of faded clinical skills and shaky confidence."

The very next day, on Good Friday itself, I found myself in a state of shock at my promptly answered prayer.

For there we all were, at one of the largest locked-down dormitory sites in Singapore.

What I thought would be a quick look-see recce trip quickly became a full-on mobile clinic and swab set-up.

My mentor, fully aware of the internal travail within me, smiled at me benevolently and passed me a set of personal protective equipment – mask, gown, goggles and all.

"Me?" I looked at him incredulously.

"You and I are the only doctors here."

Melting under the steamy heat of the protective gown under my foggy goggles and feeling slightly faint under the suffocating N95, I felt God's cool refreshing touch as I felt Him say: "Your prayer is answered. To be useful. And better still, at the frontline."

On the way home, I wept inconsolably.

GOD AT THE FRONTLINE

Putting my shoes outside our door, skirting in sideways so I wouldn't touch anything, asking my husband to bring me a change of clothes and bleach in a bucket so I wouldn't risk passing on the virus to our children, I continued to cry in the shower.

As I washed my hair and feet from tears and sweat, I remembered Jesus' death on the cross and what it represents – total surrender.

I remembered that what God requires is not capability but availability, surrender and obedience. While the world champions vessels of might and power, God looks for broken ones, eager to be refashioned for fitful use in the Master's hands.

Like the widow with two mites was I with my meagre offering of faded clinical skills, shaky confidence and clinical trauma complex.

Yet, God did not despise the widow. He loved and embraced her offering.

"In these unprecedented times, we are all in the frontline, with Him fronting the battle for us."

That Good Friday, God smashed my inadequacy and self-doubt. My mentor texted me that night: "You still have much to offer, Wai Jia."

Within a few days, great acceleration took place. Re-training and deployment opportunities were opened to me. I made meaningful connections between organisations to help the migrant workers. Cliff gave me his full support, in spite of his own condition.

I am learning that God looks at our offering very differently from the way we do.

However useless or worthless we may feel about ourselves, however ashamed we may feel about what we have to offer, God cherishes that we might have "put in more than all the others" when we give it with all our hearts.

Wai Jia with husband, Cliff, and their two daughters aged three and one.

I am learning that when He calls us to the frontline, whether it's managing the outbreak at the migrant dormitories, or opening our homes to the homeless, or helping our elderly neighbours with groceries, we can be sure that God Himself is at the frontline already, simply inviting us to experience the joy of service

In these unprecedented times, we are all at the frontline, with Him fronting the battle for us.

No offering is too small. See you at the frontline.

◆ **Text by Dr Tam Wai Jia**

Work

Her darkest moments prepared F&B CEO Jocelyn Chng to steer through COVID-19

During the current economic uncertainty of COVID-19, business decisions that once drew criticism have turned into lifelines for Chng's companies. "I don't know the purpose (of COVID), but I fear nothing because He says He will never leave nor forsake us." (Hebrews 13:5) All photos courtesy of Jocelyn Chng.

At age 21, she lost her father. At 37, she was widowed – just eight months after her beloved grandmother passed on suddenly. Naysayers disparaged her abilities and innovations. Contractors made off with her money. She also saw the ravages of the Severe Acute Respiratory Syndrome (SARS) on her business.

Award-winning businesswoman Jocelyn Chng has seen God's grace in pulling her out of her deepest hours of loss and pain.

It is an understatement to say that F&B CEO Jocelyn Chng has experienced more than her fair share of life challenges in her 53 years.

She was just a second-year student at the National University of Singapore when her father passed away after a prolonged battle with colon cancer. While juggling studies, she took over the flailing family business to help her mum feed her five siblings.

But she sees redemption in each soul-wrenching episode.

"I don't know the purpose but I fear nothing because He says: 'I am with you always.'"

"God showed a lot of mercy and grace. He helped me pull through. As I was seeing the impossible, God reminded me He was there in my darkest moment," said Chng, managing director of Sin Hwa Dee, known for its sauces and cooking mixes. She is also CEO of JR Group, an international food manufacturing and F&B company she started with her late husband.

She knows God will be no different in the current COVID-19 pandemic.

She looks to the bible verse in her room: "I will never leave you nor forsake you." (Hebrews 13:5)

"I don't know the purpose, but I fear nothing because He says: 'I am with you always'.

"As I'm telling you this, tears are rolling down because I've really experienced this again and again," she told *Salt&Light*.

INNOVATIVE LIFELINES

During the current economic uncertainty of COVID-19, Chng's business decisions that once drew detractors have turned into lifelines for her companies. In particular, her hot food vending machine business.

"People didn't believe in it. But I kept believing the vision even when they didn't."

In 2003, while at a trade fair, her late husband Richard Wong caught on to the idea of bringing hot food vending machines to Singapore.

Jocelyn with husband Richard and their three sons (*left to right*) Joel, Emmanuel, and Noel. Their sons are now 22, 18 and 25 respectively. Richard passed away in February 2004.

In 2016 – more than a decade later – Chng opened Singapore's first vending machine café with a cluster of six vending machines that dispensed everything from drinks and snacks to cooked meals and desserts.

In the years between genesis and fruition of her husband's dream, Chng lost him to lymphoma – within two weeks of being diagnosed.

Critics did not think hot food vending machines were sustainable on an island with an abundance of hawker centres, food courts and restaurants.

"When God opens doors, everything falls into place."

Chng had to convince manufacturers, solution providers and customers because the idea was so far out of the box.

"It was so hard for 10 years. People didn't believe in it. But I kept believing the vision even when they didn't," said Chng.

She did not know it then, but God was preparing her business for the current economic downturn. No doubt, the months since the coronavirus hit Singapore's shores have been difficult for Chng. But she maintains that they have been "exciting times".

"With eateries only doing takeouts and deliveries so expensive, people have been turning to our vending machines.

"Because of the better-than-expected business from the vending machines, we are able to get a lot of new insights into customer taste and eating patterns based on what foods they pick.

> "A lot of people say: 'Wah, you got vision!' How can I say I have vision? ... it was God who gave the vision."

The JR Group's hot food vending machines in HDB estates are bringing in more business during the season when people can no longer dine out. The ones in offices and schools have been dormant.

Jocelyn realised her vision of feeding thousands during the Circuit Breaker through heat-and-serve ready-meals.

"We are experiencing so many new things which we have not done before."

There has also been an increase in demand for the JR Group's other offerings as Singapore hunkered down to eating and cooking at home. They include Chef-in-Box cooked and chilled meals that can be easily heated, as well as Sin Hwa Dee's range of sauces and mixes.

The ready-to-eat meals were also part of Wong's vision. He had wanted to supply these not just to homes, but to hotels, restaurants and caterers as well.

"When the Circuit Breaker happened and restaurants and eateries could only offer takeout, they bought from us because many of them have limited staff and no central kitchen."

"The diversification has helped us," said Chng of the increase in demand for these products even as the catering and restaurant arms of her business are affected.

"A lot of people say: '*Wah*, you got vision!' How can I say I have vision? At that time, it was God who gave the vision.

"Now, I am seeing that it was paving the way for us to survive in this situation. It is all God's plan.

"It's very scary," she said of how wonderfully God has pulled everything together.

FOOD NETWORK

Known in the industry to be genuine, caring and friendly, Chng has always made it a point to build relationships with customers and employees. These contacts have been invaluable to her business during this season.

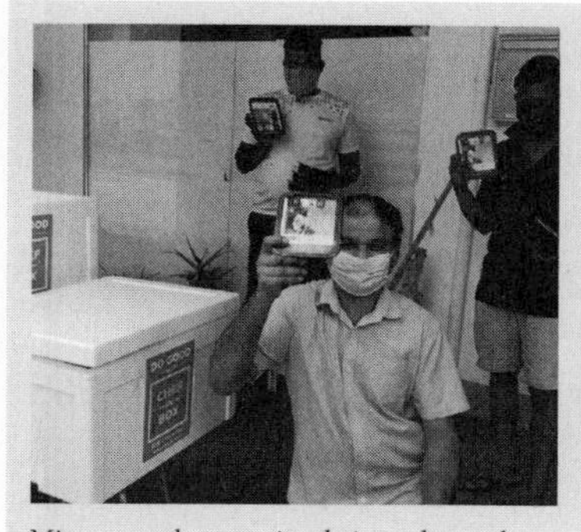

Migrant workers receive their ready-meals.

Ready-meals being dropped off at the door of someone under quarantine.

"During this crisis, I have friends calling me and asking me to cook meals for workers in the dormitories. I happen to have two Indian chefs. So I asked if they could provide suitable meals." They could.

"Another friend asked me to prepare lunches for children who had to return to school during home-based learning. Then, a partner asked us to provide meals for those being quarantined."

Friends have also been coming forward to donate meals to those in homes and shelters and getting Chng's company to prepare the food.

On her part, she offers a special discount for all sponsored meals. "When God opens doors, everything falls into place."

Years before, Chng had a dream. In it, she saw herself feeding thousands much like Jesus did with five loaves and two fishes in the Gospels (Matthew 14:13-21, Mark 6:30-44, Luke 9:10-17, John 6:1-14).

It was just shortly after her husband passed away. Chng did not quite understand what it meant, but it placed a seed of desire in her heart.

"We have always wanted to supply meals to thousands. Today, we are feeding thousands," said Chng.

"And we already had ingredients in our warehouse because were preparing for Chef-in-Box."

Her 300-strong staff, too, have taken well to this season of challenges and change.

"We spoke to the restaurant staff: 'Can you come back to the central kitchen and work? The job may be different. You may no longer be a service staff but a packer; you used to be a Japanese chef but now you have to cook rice instead.'

"They understand and they continue to work and we continue to pay them. We don't lay off anyone because they still need the job.

"It's a bit tough for the company. We don't slash their pay even if the job scope changes. We are trying to ride through the storm."

LESSONS IN LOSS

It is not the first time that Chng has had to ride through a storm created by a viral outbreak.

"I don't understand God's wisdom, but I trust His will."

"During SARS in 2003, I was fighting the battle quite alone because my sister, Kathleen, whom I now work very closely with was due to deliver her firstborn."

Chng's other siblings were too young to help in the business. "They don't even remember the SARS episode."

Even worse, her maternal grandmother passed on in April of that year. Chng was especially close to her. When her parents lost their jobs and started a small business to make ends meet, Chng's grandparents cared for her. She was just 11 years old, the eldest of six children.

Then, less than a year after her grandmother's passing, her husband died.

Chng believes the losses offer lessons that will fortify her for this season.

"I keep a prayer journal. Things that I saw as dead ends have turned around because with God nothing is impossible". (Matthew 19:26)

"I believe everything that happens has a reason. (Romans 8:28) This has kept me going."

KEEPING THE FAITH

Chng clung on to these verses when her two older sons fell ill with high fevers during the COVID-19 period.

"It started with Joel. His fever was so high he had to be warded in a hospital."

Joel had just returned from the United Kingdom and the family feared he had contracted COVID-19. It turned out to be a bacterial infection. He has since recovered.

Jocelyn with her sons (*from left to right*) Joel, Emmanuel and Noel.

Then his older brother Noel got very sick. "His fever went on for days and it was so high, almost 40 degrees," said Chng.

Again, the family feared that it was COVID-19. They sent him to the hospital.

"Things that I saw as dead ends have turned around because with God nothing is impossible."

"It turned out to be dengue. But because of the COVID-19 situation, I couldn't even visit him. His blood platelet count dropped to 12,000 when the normal range is between 150,000 to 450,000.

"He was so weak he couldn't even pick up the phone to reply my texts." The family prayed for him through their chat group.

Noel, too, has since recovered.

Through it all, Chng holds unwaveringly to the one big lesson she had learnt through her life. And which she believes will tide her through this pandemic: "God always has a purpose. We just have to wait for His timing.

It's just a matter of time before it is all over, says Chng of the pandemic. "I don't understand God's wisdom, but I trust His will."

◆Text by Christine Leow

Work

"Sighted or not, I will serve the Lord": Legally blind principal Peter Tan on seeing miracle after miracle

Queensway Secondary School principal, Peter Tan, who has seen multiple cohorts of students, is still visited by his "old boys". "It is a privilege to pray for them," he says. Photo courtesy of Darren Huang.

His door is always open. Boys would enter with equal measure of trepidation and anticipation, knowing the man within the office would be firm but kind.

There would be no escaping the truths they'd have to tell, but there would be comfort in the confession, for there would grace.

It is no secret that Peter Tan Chong Tze is first a Christ-follower before he is a school principal – a servant of God who just happens to have been called to the field of education.

From 1999 to 2017, he oversaw 18 cohorts of graduating boys from two Anglo-Chinese School (ACS) schools, first at ACS (Junior) then at ACS (Barker Road), whom he prayed over during assembly devotion every Monday morning.

"Behind closed doors, he hears them out and offers counsel. Always, he prays for them."

Alumni still seek him out. Now grown men, their stories are often replete with regret at moral lapses. Behind closed doors, he hears them out and offers counsel. Always, he prays for them.

"It is a privilege to pray," Tan says plainly. It comes so naturally to him that not being able to pray openly was a significant adjustment when he became principal at Queensway Secondary School (QSS) a little under two years ago.

The move changed nothing, however, about his habit of personal prayer. His days begin before God in the quiet of dawn, every earthly challenge a divine opportunity to inquire of God and behold His beauty (Psalm 27:4).

The perspective from that place, while often dark, has been resplendent with the miraculous.

RUN HOME!

On a Tuesday in mid-January this year, Tan, 59, found his sense of balance slipping away as he stood up from his chair in his QSS office. He was rushed to the National University Hospital where a CT scan of his brain showed a lesion indicative of a stroke.

Two days later, the results of an MRI begged to differ and he was discharged with the all-clear.

"How this can be, I do not know except that we worship a great and mighty God," he said in a "thank you" text sent to the army of kindred spirits who had gathered in cyber space to intercede for him.

It is not the only miracle he has experienced in his life.

Four years before, on the same date, his wife, Stacey, experienced acute chest pains while he was at a Father's Prayer Group meeting on the ACS(BR) campus. After her phone call to him that Saturday morning, "I sensed God telling me to run home!" and he did, said Tan in a letter of appreciation to the ACS community later.

While they were registering at the Accident and Emergency department at Tan Tock Seng Hospital, Stacey had a massive heart attack. A stent was inserted two days later when it was diagnosed that the neck of one of her main arteries was 90% blocked over a 4cm length.

Tan recalls asking a cardiologist friend: "What would have happened if it had closed?" The reply: "Then you'd be a widower *lor*."

THE AMULET

Ironically, when he was first introduced to the faith as a primary school student of ACS, he had a distinct distaste for the word "Jesus".

"The hymns always sang about Christ," he says. Steeped in another religion then, "I really resented it. I found the words very offensive, so I would refuse to sing".

In Secondary 2 he enrolled in the Boys' Brigade (BB) – being "very impressed with the BB uniform and everything" – but more so to be better informed so that he could prove Christianity a false religion.

Then: Stacey waited for Peter through the three years he was away for his undergraduate studies.

And now: Pillars of love and strength to each other, Stacey and Peter have been married 31 years. Photos courtesy of Peter Tan.

Little did he expect God to get the better of him during a Gospel outreach.

> "I just felt I had to go and get myself right with this God called Jesus Christ."

"During the altar call I just felt that warmth in the heart to say I need to respond to this. And it was strange, because I was wearing (an amulet). I was asking God, 'How can I go up? I have this.'

"And then I just felt I had to go and get myself right with this God called Jesus Christ."

That night, he removed all the religious ornaments he had worn since childhood. Mark 1:35, which says that Jesus prayed alone very early in the morning, was instructive, and he began to wake up early to read his Bible "for what it was", by torchlight in the one room his immediate family shared in his grandparents' house.

He avoided the religious rituals he'd once spearheaded as the eldest grandson of a traditional Chinese family and, over time, his once-hot temper simmered away.

These developments did not go unnoticed, and when he finally broached the subject of baptism with his formidable grandmother, she surprised him by saying "okay", adding: "Maybe you should bring your cousins to church, too."

JUST IN TIME

After serving his National Service, Tan saw himself with a future in the mission field.

But following a mountaintop experience in Sarawak grooming young Iban Christians as leaders, he found himself in a valley with Luke 14:28-31: "Make sure you have enough resources before you build your tower. Don't go into battle with your enemy if you don't have enough resources."

"If You open that door, I will become a teacher and be salt and light to the schools in Singapore."

"I remember I was driving along East Coast Parkway – I'd borrowed my grandparents' car – and those words came to me," says Tan. "I pulled up along the road shoulder and read (the passage), and God really spoke and said, 'You are not ready.' "

Tan had also considered being a teacher, and so he applied to the then-Institute of Education (IE), pledging to God: "If You open that door, I will become a teacher and be salt and light (Matthew 5:13-16) to the schools in Singapore until such time as You call me for mission work again."

The IE programme in the early 1980s was a teacher-in-training scheme, and Tan was assigned to his alma mater. He set his sights on a university degree and applied to study physical education and fitness management overseas.

The best is yet to be: Prophetic words given to others of a new wineskin confirmed Peter Tan's own sense that God was calling him to leave ACS(BR) at the end of 2017. Photo by Kevin Kwok.

Boys to men, they still seek their former principal out: The 12th Company of the Boys' Brigade are a brotherhood for life. Photo courtesy of Darren Huang.

It was an "audacious" move on his part, he says, because he had neither scholarship nor independent funding, and a teacher's pay was then only $600 a month.

He supplemented his income by giving private tuition, and also applied for the TW Hinch scholarship administered by ACS Old Boys' Association (ACSOBA), which amounted to $1,000 a year.

How he managed to pool together enough money to attend the University of Texas in Austin eludes him. "I have no idea," he shakes his head, laughing.

"Honestly. If I were to do the sums, it wouldn't add up. But I prayed and I had the peace to do all that I did."

The Ministry of Education's (MOE) take on his bid to go overseas was a definitive "no".

"If I were to do the sums, it wouldn't add up. But I prayed and I had the peace to do all that I did."

"The strange thing was, they sent a replacement to take my place as a teacher."

In faith, Tan bought his air ticket and told his students he was leaving. "I told them, 'This Friday is my last Friday in school.' The students were very nice, they did their own farewell for me and all."

That same Friday afternoon, he received word that MOE had approved his studies. "God is always just in time," he exclaims in amazement. He left for the US two days later.

◆**Text by Emilyn Tan**

"Unless we look after others, we cannot get out of this crisis": CEO Arthur Kiong on running a business amidst COVID

Inspired by his daily devotions, Arthur Kiong introduced Daily Dose in the hospitality group: Before every shift, staff take 20 minutes to visit one of 11 attributes forming the acronym ACTS OF GRACE. Kiong (*left*) having a meal with the team. All photos courtesy of Far East Hospitality.

He started his working life hawking slimming products to beauty salons when he didn't do well enough to get into university – a possibility he had never considered.

Later, he would trip into a career as a radio DJ, which would make him a household name. But then switch off that microphone to start at the bottom rung of the hospitality ladder. (He was a greeter at Italian restaurant, Prego.)

God showed him that good business and doing good in business are not mutually exclusive.

In his 34 years in the hospitality industry, veteran hotelier Arthur Kiong, 60, has battled conflict and catastrophes: The Gulf War. Severe Acute Respiratory Syndrome (SARS). 9/11. All of them radiated shock waves that brought hotel occupancy to record lows.

Now the world is facing its greatest challenge yet: COVID-19, which slammed shut international borders and, with it, many tourism-dependent businesses.

Yet Far East Hospitality, where Kiong is CEO, has managed to stay profitable and maintain staff salaries.

The Singapore-grown organisation has a portfolio of nine hotel brands, over 95 (and counting) serviced residences and apartment hotels, and more than 15,500 rooms in eight countries across Asia, Australasia and Europe.

Kiong tells *Salt&Light* how God showed him that good business and doing good in business are not mutually exclusive.

WHAT KIND OF CHALLENGES DID COVID THROW AT YOUR GROUP?

We got wind early on that the government needed facilities for quarantine, swabs in isolation and stay-home-notices. We struggled. We were thinking that we had other customers to take care of. And if we were to be involved in quarantine, there may be a stigma attached to us. But the pivot in this crisis was: Where can we make the biggest social impact? And how can we be of service to as many people as possible?

We looked upon it as a sense of national duty to support the government by committing as many hotels and as many rooms as possible.

> "The pivot in this crisis was: How can we be of service to as many people as possible?"

At that time, we thought it was this huge sacrifice that we were making. But it turned out to be a huge blessing because that was the only business available. We found out very soon that nobody could come into the country, so there was no one to offend, no one to impress.

That allowed us to be profitable through the crisis. And our organisation managed to maintain everyone's pay, and we did not lay anybody off. Which is a huge blessing. But we never started out using that as a strategy; it came as a result.

What we did for one reason turned out to be the best thing that we could do.

There was an element of divine intervention in there. I'm thanking the good Lord that none of our staff has contracted the disease so far. We managed to keep everyone safe. We have been incredibly blessed.

DID YOUR EXPERIENCE WITH 9/11 AND SARS PREPARE YOU FOR COVID?

Yes, in the way that I know how the story will end. The good Lord is in charge, and we will get out of the other side fine. I am able to assure those I lead that we will be fine, and in order to derive this outcome, let me chapter the various phases and what we must do in relation to what's happening in the marketplace.

Having gone through 9/11 and SARS taught me this particular process: The situation will get worse before it gets better. It is not going to end anytime soon; it will probably end some time next year. It will end when a vaccine or public confidence returns.

> "Societies that are united, loving and considerate to others will get out of this better and faster."

So what will happen between then and now? At some time, the domestic market and the regional market will open before the international market.

In the short term, we need to assure our staff that we are doing tangible things to keep them safe and we have their well-being at heart.

For the long term, we need to see how we can use this crisis to transform our brand and to emerge much stronger.

When you have such a definitive action plan, and are able to anticipate the market, your people pay attention and listen to you. They will be able to judge for themselves: Will it come to pass or not? On a scale of one to 10, how often are you right? And when you have proven to be able to navigate (through the crisis) and are right more often than you are wrong, it builds confidence, it builds morale. And it gives everyone a sense of belief in what you're doing.

WHAT IS YOUR MESSAGE THROUGHOUT THIS CRISIS?

This crisis is somewhat like the Tower of Babel, if you were to look at it in a philosophical way:

1 We don't control our own destiny; we are subject to forces that are beyond yourself.
2 It is an opportunity to reset our priorities.

Unless we look after others, we cannot get out of this crisis by ourselves. So for example, you're wearing a mask not just to protect yourself. You are wearing one to protect others: I protect you, you protect me. And if you love thy neighbour as yourself, you'll get through this. Societies that are selfish and believe in "my freedom above all else" will suffer.

Societies that are united, loving and considerate to others will get out of this crisis better and faster.

So having been through 9/11 and SARS, COVID doesn't scare me.

The crisis has allowed us to do some really wonderful things that we'll see the dividends of when we come out of it.

HAS THE CRISIS OPENED UP NEW OPPORTUNITIES?

We'll be seeing a world that is a lot more sensitive to quality tourism and sustainability.

I would argue that there is a levelling of the playing field for a regional chain in comparison to an international chain. This provides us with a tremendous opportunity to grow overseas.

Following Christ is integrated in everything that we do and not just reserved for certain days of the week.

Previously, when competing with the internationally branded players, the regional player is somewhat lacking in its distribution, and size of its customer base. But post-COVID, hotel owners are looking for operators that have regional strength rather than international distribution because the world has become more bifurcated. This presents opportunities for us to expand into new geographies and new types of businesses, such as resorts, spas, and our own brand of restaurants.

It's also given us the opportunity to reset and think about how we're going to create better paying jobs for Singaporeans, because moving forward, the quota on foreign labour will be tightened. To excite Singaporeans to join the hospitality industry, we have to create jobs that they desire. And in order to do that, we have to think of how we can leverage on innovation and technology to transform our style of operations.

We are also partnering local businesses to create an experience to make the brands we run come alive, and to create products that are different, exciting and extraordinary.

So when you stay at The Barracks Hotel on Sentosa, you can go on a private yacht cruise of the Southern Islands. We partner with Darren Lim, a yacht owner who happens to be a celebrity. So it's a bit of a talking factor and that will be appreciated because Singaporeans recognise him.

Staying at our Village Hotel Bugis, we'll take you on a trip to a *kelong* where you can fish. We'll cook the fish for you, and you can enjoy a lunch of what you caught at the *kelong* with your family. It's not what Singaporeans do every day.

Post-COVID, I think these products will have relevance to tourists who want to enjoy something truly authentic and different from the same-old same-old.

If it weren't for this COVID-19 reset, when would we have the opportunity to say: Let's go into new business streams? When would we have the time to sit down and say: Let's redesign our jobs so that we can attract Singaporeans for tourism to be more sustainable?

BESIDES STAFF MEETINGS, WHERE DO YOU GET YOUR IDEAS?

From my one-hour daily morning walks communing with God.

Walking 10,000 steps or swimming a kilometre is the best time to pray, to meditate. And it's not as if there's a conscious effort to try and get ideas, but it's through these processes that one finds inspiration here and there.

I used to take my swim in the middle of the day to kill three birds with one stone:

1 Not be tempted to have lunch, so that's good for my weight.
2 When you're swimming 40 laps, there's nothing to do but to meditate and pray and recite verses.
3 You get your exercise done.

I don't swim so much now because it's very inconvenient – you have to book a lane, and a lane is not always available. During this pandemic, walking is the more efficient exercise.

HOW DO YOU MANAGE YOUR TIME AS A BUSY CEO?

In the job that I do, it's virtually impossible to practise work-life balance, to say that, for the next two days, I'm just switching off.

> "Work-life integration means trying to commune with God and experience His presence multiple times in a day."

In my role, I'm on 24/7 because it's an operational business, and I need to be involved. I don't need to micromanage, but I need to be accessible for my team.

I believe in work-life integration. So, in the course of my day, it's how I take time off to enrich my mind, how I take time off to pray.

I am a firm believer that communing with God is not dedicated to only a time in the morning or before one sleeps. Work-life integration means trying to experience God's presence multiple times in a day. Before we partake in a meal, before we go into a meeting, before we communicate an idea ... we say a silent prayer.

And there's time to observe and be still and know that He is God. Following Christ is integrated in everything that we do.

HOW DO YOU BRING CHRISTIAN PRINCIPLES INTO MANAGEMENT?

I'm very lucky because Philip Ng, owner of Far East Organisation that I work for, is a stalwart Christian. And he has provided a template and the platform that allows us to do the work we do. He has three principles:

1 **We are all stewards and we are servant leaders**. And nothing we have, we actually own. We are given this limited time to do the best we can to grow what we have been given. So we have been given talents – wealth (in the Bible, a talent is a unit of money) or talents that we are bestowed with. How do we use and grow what we are given?

2 **We all need more ministering and less administering.**
3 **We're here to do good business, as well as do good in business.**

I think these are very powerful. The Christian ethos is embedded in the way we conduct business.

For the hospitality side of the business that I am in charge of, I identified 11 behavioural traits that I hold dear. They form the acronym ACTS OF GRACE.

Attitude : We are responsible for our own well-being.
Customer : Do unto others what you want others to do to you.
Teamwork : Not only must you know your role, but you must know the role of your neighbour. So that you can step in and help him, just as he can step in to help you. To walk a mile in someone else's shoes is very important. I always say that teamwork is not a relay but a game of football.
Savviness : We don't want to be corporate Pharisees, where you do everything right, but you're not doing the right thing.
Observation : To observe the unspoken needs of others.
Fulfilment : What can we do to help our customers and ourselves be more fulfilled?
Gratitude : In everything give thanks. (1 Thessalonians 5:18).
Responsive : So when you send me an email, you'll get an immediate response from me. Even if I can't give you an answer, I'll tell you that I'm working on it.
Anticipate : Think and plan ahead.
Change : Change is constant; find a better way to do your job. Evolve.
Engender trust: Underpromise, overdeliver.

These 11 behavioural standards are embedded in everything that we do.

> "We don't want to be corporate Pharisees, where you do everything right, but you're not doing the right thing."

Inspired by *Our Daily Bread* devotions, we have a system called Daily Dose: In every hotel, in every department, before every shift, everyone gets together to huddle for 20 minutes, and we visit one of these attributes. We talk about what we can do better in behavioural standards.

We are also very careful as an organisation that embraces Christian values not to make believers of other faiths amongst us – and they are the majority – feel disenfranchised. So, we are spreading the Gospel through tangible things we do: How we treat each other, how we exercise compassion, how we are not nickel-and-diming our customer, how we go beyond what is necessary, and give the benefit of the doubt, how we turn the other cheek. So these systems allow us to live out our Christian walk through our work.

IS THIS NATURAL FOR YOU?

I'm not a naturally humble, gentle type of guy. I'm a naturally take charge and let-me-tell-you-my-opinion kind of guy. But I try to control my natural overbearing Type A personality by wanting to be an obedient servant of Christ. I don't know whether I'm succeeding or not.

Kiong (*right*) and his Quincy Hotel team receiving the Best Experience Hotel award by the Singapore Tourism Board in 2017.

But I'm grateful for a very cohesive and very loyal team that has been with me for a very long time. And I think, at the end of the day, one is judged by the fruits of the Spirit (Galatians 5:22-23).

One has to ask oneself: Is there love, peace and joy? Is

there kindness, is there patience? If, generally speaking, these fruits exist in the work environment that I'm responsible for, then I would be judged by the fruits.

And the fruits of our labour must be attractive enough for others to ask: Why are you different? What is your philosophy? Who do you worship?

And that's the way I want to live my life.

◆**Text by Gemma Koh**

Work

When SARS pushed an infectious diseases doctor toward God

Dr Leong in his office at Rophi Clinic; "rophi" is a Hebrew word which means "to heal"

An epidemic that caused a national crisis and international alarm? Hardly anyone would consider *that* an intervention of grace by a sovereign God.

But 50-year-old infectious diseases specialist and SARS (Severe Acute Respiratory Syndrome) victim, Dr Leong Hoe Nam, is not just *anyone*; he is a man whose excruciating experience with SARS while quarantined in Germany was a key step towards knowing his Father's love.

Many of us would remember 2003 as the year of SARS. Stories of the shared experiences in pain and joy have been told; the actions of heroes honoured, the lives of victims remembered. But Dr Leong's remarkable story towards God is one that few have heard.

A MYSTERIOUS DISEASE

In 2003, Dr Leong and his wife, Dr Lim Hong Huay, were infected with SARS and quarantined in Frankfurt, Germany, for two-and-a-half weeks.

It turned out that Dr Leong had contracted the virus while treating the first SARS patient in Singapore – "patient no. 1". He happened to be the infectious diseases doctor on-call the day she was admitted. At the time, her illness was a mystery.

No one knew about SARS then. The working diagnosis of her illness was "atypical pneumonia" – which only meant that she had an unknown lung infection.

But Dr Leong came down with a high fever and severe body pain – symptoms he attributed to dengue. After plenty of rest and fluids, his fever subsided. So he and his wife decided to go ahead with their plans to attend a conference in New York. Two days into his trip, he fell ill again.

This time, it was he who was diagnosed with "atypical pneumonia".

Before Dr Leong and his wife left for Singapore, he called a trusted colleague in Singapore to update him on his condition. By then, patient no. 1's illness had been identified and the term "SARS" had just been coined.

Unbeknownst to him, Dr Leong's phone call would set off a chain reaction which eventually led to his being quarantined in Frankfurt, Germany.

SUFFERING THROUGH SARS

Dr Leong suffered badly from the effects of the SARS virus. He recalled: "I had to cope with hacking bouts of cough. Every single attempt to adjust my posture would result in my coughing out blood."

Even breathing was difficult. "One evening, I tried to take deeper and deeper breaths but to no avail. I felt suffocated – as if the air had no oxygen – even though I had on a full-face 100% oxygen mask.

"The sensation of breathlessness was terrifying."

He said: "I was not a Christian then but I was not afraid of death, because all of us will die. I just knew I had to avoid mechanical ventilation if I wanted to keep the odds in my favour."

A LOVE THAT PURSUES

He soon overcame the virus and started to recover. But he faced a bigger problem: Inactivity.

Dr Leong, a self-declared workaholic, was stuck in a German hospital with nothing to stimulate his active mind. He was someone who needed to be doing or reading something *constantly*.

"I'm busy. *Always* busy. Work to me is like cheese to a rat. Give me work, I will do. Give me a treadmill, I will run."

"That Bible was the only English text that I could get my hands on."

Back in 2003, mobile phones were still rudimentary and most people still used a dial-up connection for the Internet. Getting hold of something to read in English was almost impossible. The Winter Olympics was showing on the television, but there was only so much figure skating he could endure watching.

But his wife, who was a very young Christian then, had gotten hold of an English bible. She asked him to read it since there was not much else to do.

Today, Dr Leong laughs as he recalls his desperation: "I was a reasonably fervent believer of another faith, but that Bible was the only English text that I could get my hands on!"

His wife suggested that he start with the Gospel of Luke since they were both physicians, as was Luke. Dr Leong obliged, even though he says now that he thinks the Gospel of John would have been much easier to start with.

By the time he was done, Dr Leong was confronted with the person of Jesus: "Jesus was either an incredibly charismatic and influential leader with a bunch of fools for followers, or there is indeed a true God and Jesus *is* the Son of God."

Dr Leong could not decide if the God of the Bible was real ... or not.

He and his wife eventually returned to Singapore and fought in the ongoing battle of the SARS crisis.

On May 31, 2003, Singapore was declared SARS-free, and life went back to normal for the couple. Dr Leong was not yet convinced of God's truth. But he felt no pressing reason to resolve this puzzle, so the question was left unanswered.

FINDING GOD

In 2004, Dr Leong moved to London to pursue his PhD. Life was good: Unlike his life in Singapore, he now had a lot of time on his hands. Weekend road trips out of the city were the norm.

> "If I had to go through SARS
> a hundred times over just to know the
> God whom I love, I'd do it."

At the insistence of his wife, they found the Chinese Church In London and joined a cell group. Back in Singapore, when Dr Lim first started attending church, Dr Leong had thought it was a complete waste of time. "I detested it because Sunday mornings were my precious mornings off!"

But in London, Dr Leong did not mind attending church and cell group together. In fact, he made friends with a cell member named Marcus Andrew, whose wife was a doctor.

Andrew answered many of Dr Leong's questions about the faith and directed him to resources on Christianity as well.

This became a crucial foundation that set the stage for his eventual conversion.

In 2006, Dr Leong was having trouble in his research – his experiments just weren't working out. And to make matters worse, he could not find anyone to ask for advice and guidance. He was well and truly stuck.

"I literally felt the warmth of God's presence."

By then, Dr Leong had heard enough about God that he decided to pray and ask for help with his work. "God, help me get my experiments working. Just help me."

Nothing happened.

Dr Leong started to get frustrated, but he kept praying. Eventually, he started to bargain with God: "OK God, I'll do it Your way. Whatever You want, I will do. But You *really* need to help me with this."

Still nothing.

Then one day, as Dr Leong was walking from the tube at Hampstead station towards his college, he prayed a different prayer.

"That's it. God, come what may, I submit to You. If the experiments work, then they work. If they don't work, I *still* submit to Your authority in my life."

"God's hand is on my work now. Without Him, all the work that I do would be useless."

Suddenly, he was embraced by God. "I literally felt the warmth of God's presence. He was hugging me! God said to me, 'You are my son, you are my beloved son.' And all my stress and anxiety about work, everything, just melted away."

Dr Leong remembers this thought clearly: "OK, it doesn't matter. Whether my experiment succeeds or not, it doesn't matter. I've got God with me now."

TWO STEPS TO FAITH

Looking back on his journey to faith, Dr Leong surmises: "If I hadn't been infected with SARS, I wouldn't have read the Bible. If I hadn't gotten away from work in Singapore, I wouldn't have known God."

He says that he is often asked if he has any regrets about SARS. The benefit of hindsight is not lost on him; time has passed but the experience is still fresh in his mind.

He takes a moment to compose himself before replying: "God is very, very, very dear to me. If I had to go through SARS a hundred times over just to know the God whom I love, I'd do it."

He recognises the painful experience of SARS as a necessary intervention and milestone in his personal journey. "If God hadn't taken me away from the distractions of work, I would never have read the Gospel of Luke."

And if he had not read the Gospel of Luke, he would never have been confronted with Jesus.

Many might believe that science and God do not mix. But while Dr Leong works hard at keeping abreast of new developments in science, he leaves room for God to intervene and guide him through every case that he takes on.

Dr Leong in his office.

In fact, he relies on God's guidance to the extent that his colleagues have been known to say that he "performs miracles" on his patients. Dr Leong attributes the good work he does to God, clarifying that it is not his brilliance but, rather, fruits of his obedience to the promptings of God.

"God's hand is on my work now. Without Him, all the work that I do would be useless."

◆ **Text by Tan Huey Ying**

Work

Malcolm Lee's Michelin secret: God's in the kitchen at Candlenut

"The restaurant is not about the awards, it is about people. It should be about making people happy," says Candlenut's Malcolm Lee (*centre*). All photos from Candlenut's Facebook page

A bout of depression so defined his future's path that Malcolm Lee openly shares what would otherwise be a closely guarded secret.

The head chef and founder of Candlenut, the world's only Michelin-starred Peranakan restaurant, Lee is candid about how his long hours took a heavy toll on him and his relationships.

"I was working so much that I was neglecting time with God, my family, friends, cell group, loved ones," the 35-year-old says. "I lost a lot of things to reach here."

"Here" is now the fourth year that Candlenut has achieved Michelin star status. It's a height he attributes to his support network of family, church friends and colleagues who rallied around him during that dark season of melancholy.

"How am I impacting their lives? How can I reflect Christ in Candlenut?"

"God sent all these people around me to make sure I was okay. Even though I was not in the right state of mind, they kept encouraging me."

Their loving words and actions redirected him back to God and prompted the questions: "What is Your plan and purposes for me? Why did you place me here?"

The answer was rooted in a reflection on his beginnings. The reason Lee wanted to be a chef in the first place was, primarily, for people – the myriad variety of people he would come into contact with, both staff and guests, at his restaurant.

It set him thinking: "How am I impacting their lives? How can I reflect Christ in Candlenut?"

As he sought God, it became clear that he was to change his restaurant's culture – unthinkable though the move might be, by industry standards.

GETTING A LIFE

At the top of Lee's list was work-life balance. His staff worked six days a week, sometimes at a stretch of more than 14 hours per day. The physical demands of manning the kitchen meant that many of them just slept in on their rest day, instead of spending time with their family and friends – a job hazard Lee was all too familiar with.

Food and beverage (F&B) industry workers hardly see their loved ones and vice versa, and this is fuel for much misunderstanding especially between couples.

"This is very common and that is usually why F&B staff are very frustrated. It is not them but the environment they are in. So, as a boss, I need to change the environment."

"It is not them but the environment they are in. So, as a boss, I need to change the environment."

F&B staff cook up as much of a storm at home because of their long working hours. Hence, Malcolm Lee's efforts to make sure Candlenut's people have time for their families.

He reorganised the work week to give his staff at least two days off, even though it translated immediately into a 20 to 25% loss in manpower.

"It was painful to execute," reflects Lee, who gave his staff priority ahead of himself and spent "many hours" shaping the system. "For me to enjoy this, I need to make sure my team has it first."

Another change he implemented was a transparent pay and leave structure, which ensures his staff are compensated when they work overtime – this, in an industry notorious for short-changing its workers their fair dues.

Also, no one was to contact those on leave unless absolutely necessary. Establishing this boundary was important to Lee, as it was akin to keeping the Sabbath (Exodus 20:8-11).

CLEANING UP

Besides long hours and unfair practices, restaurant kitchens are known to be toxic places where unkind words and vulgarities can sometimes lead to fights.

Lee pronounced a ban on vulgar language in Candlenut's kitchen, encouraging his staff instead to speak nicely to one another to resolve issues (Proverbs 12:18, 15:1).

"Some of my staff think I'm crazy," he laughs. "It has taken a long time to instil this habit of speaking kindly to one another. It is only possible when one has pure intentions – sincerity, love – for others."

This Biblical tenet extends to managing errant staff too. Lee describes: "If someone has issues, most bosses/managers/sous chefs go: 'Why you so slow?! Even my grandmother works faster than you!'"

"So we sit them down, talk to them ... because we don't know what the person is going through."

But not at Candlenut. "You can come in love, patience, kindness, goodness, gentleness," says Lee, citing the fruit of the Spirit (Galatians 5:22-23).

"So we sit them down, talk to them. Some of them cannot see why I always do this, but it helps because we don't know what the person is going through. Maybe he's got some injury or some problem? We need to understand."

Lee also leaves encouraging words and Bible verses on the kitchen's schedule as his little way of ministering to his staff.

"I write little notes for them too, like how my church friends always write them for me. Sometimes my staff find it quite funny, why I would write little notes for them," he chortles. "These notes take a lot of time *leh*."

He has also told his staff: "Anything, just tell me. If you have any problem, just tell me" – because he sees himself as not just their boss, but as their mentor and family too.

It's his way of loving his people like Christ loves the Church.

Good food is better with great friends: Flanking Malcolm Lee are (*left to right*) Willin Low of Wild Rocket, Wayne Liew of KEK Seafood and Andrei Soen of Park Bench Deli, who took part in Candlenut's "8 years, 8 Hands" anniversary dinner on April 11, 2018.

HEARTY AROMA

Many of his staff have told him that they have never worked in a restaurant environment like his, where staff take care of and support each other like a big family and iron out issues calmly.

Even guest chefs have asked: "How come it is so different in your kitchen?"

Lee's take: "When you enter a kitchen, you can sense the energy. If it is toxic, you can feel its tiredness, its frustration. And conversely, you can feel a bright kitchen as well. You can see it on people's faces, the energy, the way they talk to you.

"I wouldn't have been able to change it without God's principles."

"I think we have that and people can sense it. And then I get the opportunity to share the whole story of why I'm changing the culture in Candlenut, how it changes the staff's mentality and what I'm basing my decisions on."

Turning the prevalent restaurant culture on its head required sacrifices and a dying to self for Lee. "It is very hard. Candlenut's doing what restaurants are supposed to and more.

"I wouldn't have been able to change it without God's principles."

Scripture guides how he runs the restaurant – something, he readily admits, he is still in the midst of learning and implementing.

At the end of the day, Candlenut is less about its Michelin-star distinction and all about the lives that it gets to touch.

"How do you cook good food for people? When your staff is happy to work here and your loved ones happy to support you, this naturally translates into better food and service, which leads to happy guests.

"When these click, it is beautiful," Lee smiles.

"The restaurant is not about the awards, it is about people. It should be about making people happy."

◆Text by Geraldine Tan

Under one roof: Malcolm Lee and his Candlenut family celebrating the restaurant winning a Michelin star for the fourth year running.

Work

"We were meant to be here": SARS doctor who arrived in Singapore just before the outbreak

Dr Lim Poh Lian on a WHO outbreak mission.

"The symptoms of love were the same as those of cholera." – Gabriel Garcia Marquez*

It was a quote from one of the books, *Love in the Time of Cholera*, on Dr Lim Poh Lian's crowded bookshelf.

And unbeknownst to her, she was about to learn what it truly meant to see love and disease meet in one cataclysmic clash.

TRAGEDY AND HEROISM

A family portrait taken in January 2003, shortly before the SARS outbreak hit home.

Dr Lim was a young mother when she arrived in Singapore to work for the first time in 2003. Malaysian-born and American citizens, she and her husband, Yap Vong Hin, stepped off the plane with three young children in tow, including a toddler from China, adopted barely a month before.

She also happened to be an infectious diseases doctor.

Within three weeks of starting work in Singapore, SARS hit. And her young family found themselves in the eye of the hurricane.

"It was probably the hardest six months of my life," says Dr Lim soberly. "We were fighting for our lives, working 80 hours a week in outbreak conditions. Apart from patients, I was taking care of doctors and nurses who were dying. I had never worked here before and it was a very harsh introduction to Singapore.

"There was a lot tragedy but also a lot of heroism. It was an incredible privilege to work alongside all those people."

"But I remember, in the middle of all that, walking into the hospital auditorium one day where they'd called a prayer meeting and seeing all these believers who were praying – people who had come from the community, from churches, to stand with us and pray for us. It was just such an incredible experience of grace in the midst of crisis.

"There was a real bond among the doctors and nurses and helpers who were working together – people who were basically standing in the gap to fight the outbreak."

The poignant stories of courage and dedication left a deep impression on Dr Lim.

One of them was of Dr Alexandre Chao, who voluntarily cut short his leave in the US to fly back and join his colleagues in the fight against the virus.

The vascular surgeon, who was the only son of the late forensic expert Chao Tzee Cheng, was one of the 33 people in Singapore who succumbed to the virus.

Dr Chao's wife, Dr Koh Woon Puay, remembers his "unwavering decision to return as soon as he heard the news about the outbreak in SGH".

"He advised me against going to Toronto for a research award and presentation at that time (Canada was also in the midst of a SARS outbreak), but never did he once doubt his own decision to return to the frontline of danger," she said in an interview with Singapore General Hospital (SGH).

"I remember there were weeks when I would go to church and just sit in the pew, crying," recalls Dr Lim. "During the week you're sort of doing, doing, doing, and you're just keeping it all together. And when you have a chance to sit down and reflect, everything just catches up with you and you just grieve for the people who are dying.

"There was a lot tragedy but also a lot of heroism. It was an incredible privilege to work alongside all those people."

GOD IN THE MIDST OF CRISIS

Matters escalated even further when Dr Lim's father took ill in Malaysia.

"My father was in poor health and he underwent surgery in Malaysia. Although I had planned to take leave during his surgery, I couldn't go through with it because I was working the outbreak here. He had a post-op complication and died.

"It was very hard, because we were in the middle of the SARS outbreak and when I went to his wake and funeral, my relatives, who had known me for 37 years, refused to shake my hand."

> "I found that the only thing more stigmatising than being an AIDS doctor is being a SARS doctor."

Some might call the Yaps' move to Singapore untimely, even unfortunate. But that thought never crossed the Yaps' mind.

"God was very much in the midst of it all. We had a very, very clear sense that the timing was providential. I felt like a fireman who had been training all my life and then 9/11 happened," says Dr Lim.

"I was literally only the sixth infectious diseases doctor who was at the hospital taking care of SARS patients."

Yap agrees. "In fact, we felt that we were here at the right time. Even though so many things were happening, we never looked back. Obviously there were concerns, but you just have to trust in God."

In fact, Dr Lim, who had studied and worked in the US for over 20 years, had been praying to move back to Asia.

"We had a very clear sense that we were called to be here and, as hard as it was, if this was where we were called, this was where we were meant to be.

"I was working with AIDs patients before this, and then I found that the only thing more stigmatising than being an AIDS doctor is being a SARS doctor!"

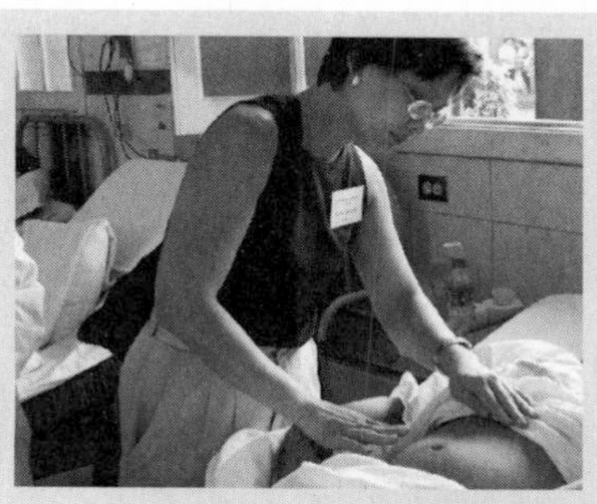

Taking a tropical medicine course in Peruvian hospitals in 2005.

MEDICINE AS MISSIONS

The calmness with which Dr Lim recalls this traumatic period of Singapore's history – and, more poignantly, her own personal history – belies her tremendous faith and courage.

"SARS is not voodoo or black magic. It is an infection," says Dr Lim, who received her BA in Biochemistry from Harvard, medical degree from Columbia and Masters of Public Health from Tulane.

She had dreamt of being a doctor since she was eight, after reading about Edward Jenner, Louis Pasteur and other pioneers in medicine.

"There was so much fear, despair and stigma for AIDS patients that I felt Christians needed to be in the frontlines."

"I was in medical school in New York City from 1987 to 1991, right when HIV AIDS was peaking. So death was very real. We got splashed with the blood of HIV patients in the course of our work, so we had already faced that fear.

"But I had a very clear sense I was called into medicine and God equipped me and gave me the opportunity to be in medicine."

At Urbana, a student missions conference, which she attended at the age of 19, she made a commitment to serve the Lord overseas (outside of America, where she was studying at the time).

So during the long years of medical training in the US, she turned down offers for a US green card because she felt called elsewhere.

In her final year as a medical student, she worked for two months in Zimbabwe at a mission hospital.

When Dr Lim was considering medical missions in Africa, she spent two months as a medical student in Zimbabwe in 1991.

"There, I felt the Lord was calling me, not to Africa, but back to Asia. That's how we ended up in Singapore in 2003."

Medicine, to the stalwart doctor, was equivalent to missions.

"I see my current work as being a tent-maker, like Paul. I went into infectious diseases because I found the area intellectually fascinating and I also see my work as worship – loving God with all my mind.

"God has given us not a spirit of fear but a spirit of love and power and a sound mind

(2 Timothy 1:7). And we want to love God with all our heart, soul, mind and strength (Matthew 22:37)."

She knew that her specialty would be particularly useful in developing countries where people still struggle with infections such as tuberculosis, malaria and other tropical diseases.

"Public health allows a focus for the needs of poor and marginalised communities. HIV was the struggle of our time. There was so much fear, despair and stigma for HIV AIDS patients that I felt Christians needed to be in the frontlines, caring for people with HIV infection.

"The grace and truth of Christ are most needed in the darkest places."

She adds with conviction: "The reality of being a doctor is that you have a duty to care for your patients, even at risk to yourself. I don't think of it as heroic. Someone has to walk with patients through the valley of the shadow of death. And the reality is that we are human and some of us will succumb. In a sense, you can't love your own life more than the duty that God has given you."

THROUGH THE VALLEY OF SHADOW

If the Yap family thought that the worst was over with SARS, it was not. Another crisis was to hit the family.

Four years ago, Dr Lim was diagnosed with breast cancer.

"My mother had breast cancer, so I had been getting regular mammograms. But it was still a shock," reveals Dr Lim, who subsequently underwent surgery, chemotherapy and radiation therapy.

"Cancer is like an earthquake where you find out whether the foundations on which you've built your life are solid, or whether everything comes crashing down.

"With cancer, you find out whether the foundations on which you've built your life are solid, or whether everything comes crashing down."

"I came through it with a renewed sense of the love of Christ, who walked with me through my valley of the shadow of death.

"For me, cancer was a sobering reminder that we need to realise our days are numbered in God's book of life, and we need to apply our hearts to living wisely."

As an infectious diseases specialist, she is no stranger to mortality.

"My medical training in New York, Boston and New Orleans took place at a time when we were fighting for the lives of our AIDS patients. During SARS, I saw medical and nursing colleagues and patients, many my age or younger, dying in the outbreak.

"I've seen people of all ages and walks of life get sick and die – some suddenly, some after a long illness.

"I have always tried to live life as fully as I can, because I know I will have to give an account to the Lord for what I have done with the time and gifts He entrusted to me."

"SUCCESS IS TO LOVE GOD"

Through crisis after crisis, the Yap family's faith has kept them strong and unwavering in their belief in God's goodness.

"God has been more than good to me.
I know I can trust Him with my dearest ones."

"Definitely our faith has affected the way we have brought up our children," says Yap, an architect who is now stay-at-home dad to their four children. "Poh Lian has told them many times, 'I'm not afraid of dying. But if I should die, these are the things that you should be aware of and be concerned about.' So that was one way of demonstrating faith in a real way to them.

"We also tell them that success is not defined by materialism; success is to love God. We tell them that, over and above all else, what's most important to us is for them to continue walking with

The three Yap children, none the worse for wear, after authorities declared SARS over in Singapore on May 31, 2003.

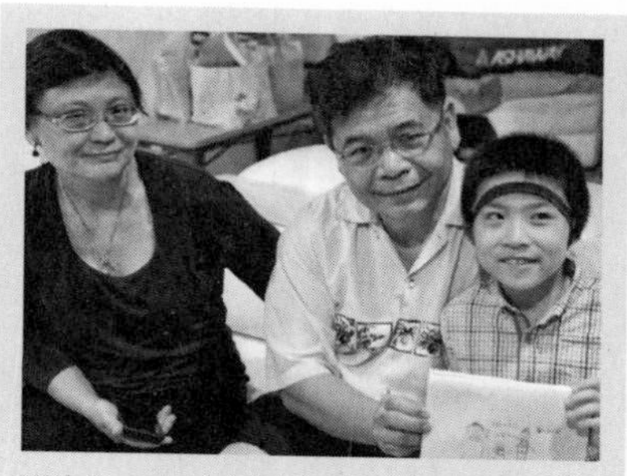

With Keyuan, shortly after he was adopted by the Yaps in early 2018.

God. And if they lose their faith, that would be the worst thing, no matter how successful they are."

Dr Lim adds, peace in her voice: "With my cancer, I realise I may not have unlimited time to transmit to our children all the life lessons I want to give them. It's a bit like an exam where you think you have two hours to answer all 100 questions, and suddenly you're told you might be given only 60 minutes.

"I continue to make preparations so that if anything happens to me or to Vong, our affairs are in good order and our children are provided for. Practicalities like wills, guardians, durable power of attorney, organising documents – these have been in place for years, but need updating now that we've added Keyuan as a child."

Keyuan, the eight-year-old whom the Yaps adopted from a Beijing orphanage just this year, has brought deep joy to the entire family, who are now Singapore permanent residents.

"With all my heart, I want to live to see my kids grow up well in the Lord. I would love to dance at their weddings and hold my grandchildren.

"But even if my life stops early, God has been more than good to me. I know I can trust Him with my dearest ones, and trust that He will love them even more than I do."

◆ **Text by Juleen Shaw**

Work

Palliative care nurses: Bedside angels to the dying and their families

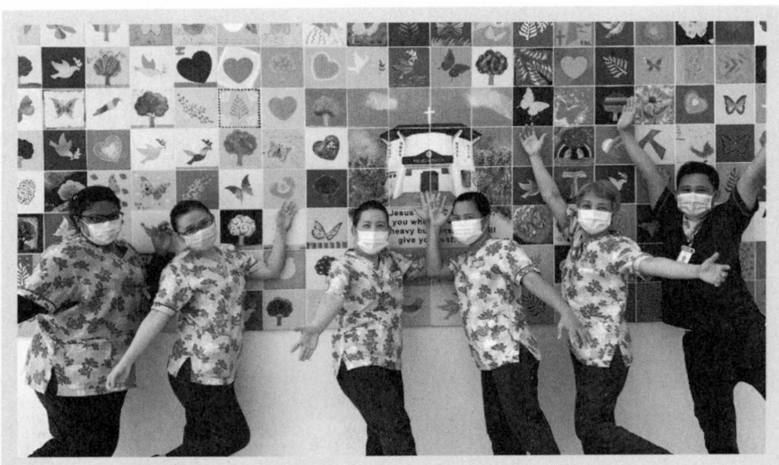

Sister Eliada (*third from left*) with her team of palliative care nurses at Assisi Hospice. For Nurses' Day 2020, Assisi has launched an "I Care For Assisi Nurses (I C.A.N)" campaign, where members of the public can read the stories of their nurses and write a note of appreciation to show their support for them: www.icareforassisinurses.sg. Photo courtesy of Assisi Hospice.

When Ng Xinhui turned 21, her 30-year-old brother was diagnosed with end-stage colon cancer. Three years later, he passed away.

In 2019, Ng turned 33 – the same age that her brother was when he died.

It was the final push she needed to enter palliative care after 13 years as a ward nurse in Singapore General Hospital's haematology department, caring for patients with blood disorders.

Palliative care has always been particularly meaningful to Ng. She knows too well the journey that awaits a patient and the loved ones as death approaches.

AGAINST THE GRAIN

Palliative medicine, which includes end-of-life care, focuses on improving the quality of life for patients with life-threatening illnesses through the prevention and relief of the illness-induced suffering.

It is a relatively new field developed in the late 1940s in Britain. The first palliative care service in Singapore was started only 35 years ago in a home for the aged where 16 beds were set aside for terminally ill patients.

Xinhui (*back row*) with her brother (*middle*) and sister (*front row*). Her brother passed away from colon cancer when she was 24 years old. She had been his main caregiver. Photo courtesy of Xinhui Ng.

The word, "palliative", throws many people off, Ng said. "There is a stigma associated with the idea of it, a resigned waiting for death to come."

But during her student attachment in palliative care, Ng recalled the impression it had made on her.

"The nurses treated the patient as a *person* – it was as simple as that."

In medicine, it is all too easy to treat patients as medical problems to be treated and "sorted out", Ng explained. What had attracted her then, was the way the nurses respected the patient and the family, taking care to uplift their spirits and gently draw out sensitive information without hurting them.

Palliative treatment is multi-dimensional and systems-focused, addressing the physical, emotional and psychosocial health of the patient, taking into account family dynamics and circumstances.

"I was awed. It's such a tough topic to talk about dying – it's really a skill," said Ng.

A RECKONING

Ng had been her brother's main caregiver in his final month as the effects of the cancer finally took its toll on him after two years of relatively good health.

> "My dad already lost his wife. And he was going to lose his only son – it was very difficult."

"It was very stressful to witness him being ill," Ng said as she recalled her turmoil and helplessness as she looked after her brother. She was still a young nurse with only a few years of experience. As his condition worsened, Ng often found herself praying that God would take him home.

Keenly aware of the distress that her father was experiencing, Ng held her emotions at bay and did not allow herself to cry at home. Her mother had passed away from the same cancer when Ng was seven.

"My dad already lost his wife. And he was going to lose his only son to the same illness," she said. "There was a lot of tension, it was very difficult."

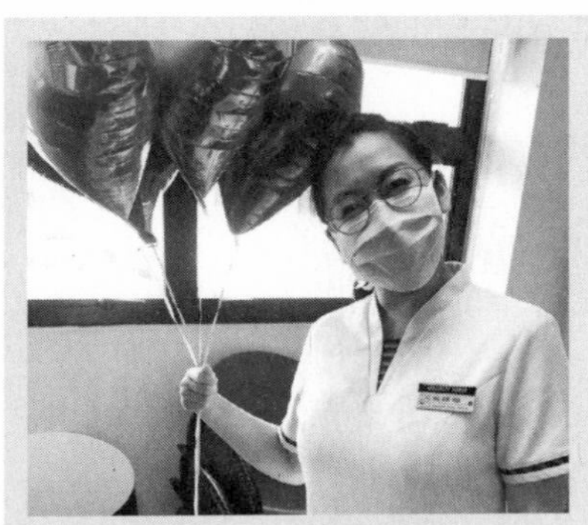

Xinhui joined the palliative care department in the National Cancer Centre of Singapore in January this year. Photo courtesy of Xinhui Ng.

At 33, as Ng reckoned with the pain of losing her brother and the brevity of life, she reconsidered her role as a nurse and her interest in palliative care.

So, after exploring various other nursing roles that included a stint at Assisi Hospice, Ng joined the palliative care department of the National Cancer Centre of Singapore (NCCS) in January this year.

A DIFFERENT AURA

The distinctive characteristics of palliative care arise from its fundamental emphasis on the consideration of the patient as a multi-dimensional being. More than 20 years earlier, Sister Eliada Yap, a ward nurse in Tan Tock Seng Hospital's surgical ward had been drawn to these very characteristics.

"They were like angels walking into the ward – their presence was so calming!"

"I noticed that they had a very different approach," she said, referring to Professor Pang Weng Sun and Dr Angel Lee, who were early practitioners in palliative care medicine in Singapore. "They were like angels walking into the ward – their presence was so calming!"

In the surgical unit, the emphasis was on the surgery and a quick recovery. When patients were deemed no longer curable, they would be referred to either of the two doctors who were part of the geriatrics department at that time. (Geriatrics was still relatively new and end-of-life care was considered a part of the specialty because of the association between death and the elderly.)

Sister Eliada Yap (*extreme left*) with the first hospital-based palliative care service team in Tan Tock Seng Hospital in 1998. It was a multi-disciplinary team consisting of doctors, therapists, medical social workers and nurses, including Dr Angel Lee (*middle, front row*). Photo courtesy of Eliada Yap/Assisi Hospice.

Professor Pang and Dr Lee would come in, take a chair and sit beside the patient to talk – sometimes, they even held patients' hands.

"When the patients see them, they are at ease and share freely ... I was very inspired!"

Yap decided to learn from them so that she could serve her patients better. At 18, Yap became a Christian and decided from then on that she did not want to become an accountant because she wanted a more "caring" profession.

"My direction in life changed. I didn't want to just sit there and look at numbers," said Yap, who became a nurse in 1988.

Almost a decade later, she was invited to join Professor Pang and Dr Lee in their newly-formed team which was the first hospital-based palliative care service in Singapore.

CONTINUITY OF CARE

The field of palliative care in Singapore has grown significantly in the last two decades with various hospices and organisations set up, either independently or within hospitals. Centred on the idea of a "good death", palliative medicine takes a multi-disciplinary approach – involving doctors, nurses, social workers and even others like music and art therapists.

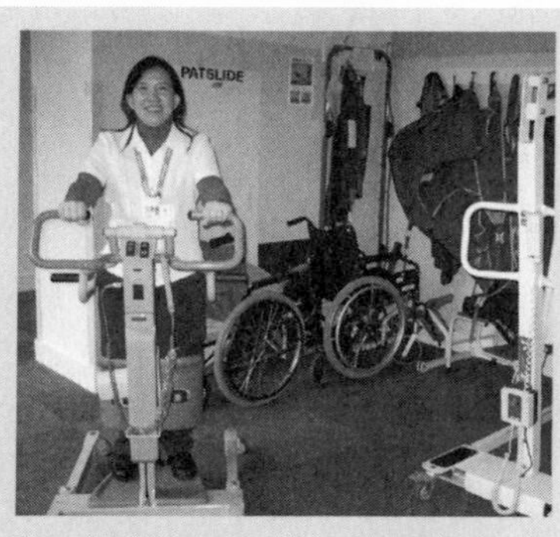

Sister Eliada Yap pursued further studies in palliative care, earning her Masters while in Melbourne, Australia. She worked there for several years before returning to Singapore. Photo courtesy of Eliada Yap/Assisi Hospice.

A patient's dignity is of priority, and care is taken to surround him or her with the warmth of human contact through loved ones and familiar faces. Helping the patient leave this world in peace, with no unfinished business, is the gold standard.

"To me, patients need not suffer when they are dying," said Yap.

Yap, who has since completed her Masters degree in palliative studies and is now the senior nurse manager at Assisi Hospice, still remembers one of her early patients. Until today, his case remains a graphic reminder of the importance of a holistic, systems-based approach.

"He was a chicken wholesale seller who had cancer of the lung. His wife was visually impaired. They had four children – his eldest had special needs," Yap said.

Having exhausted his treatment options, he was discharged to pass his last days at home. Arrangements were made and a helper was hired to help the family.

"I still remember that when I walked into his house, I saw all these green patches on the floor."

But on the second day of caregiver training, the helper arrived crying: The house was so dirty that she did not know where to start cleaning. So Yap and a medical social worker rallied two volunteers – including Yap's husband – to make a home visit. "We needed to support his helper and make it easier for her. We didn't want her to run away."

Sparing no details, Yap described the scene that they saw when they arrived. "I still remember that when I walked into his house, I saw all these green patches on the floor. They looked mouldy and I was wondering what it was.

"I realised that – my gosh – it's actually the sputum of the patient."

The phlegm that he had spat out between coughing fits had not been cleaned up – his wife's severe visual impairment meant that she could not see the patches.

"Right there, I tell you, I wondered if this is what it would take for me to prepare a patient to go home," Yap said honestly, as she shared about the thick grime that covered the walls of the kitchen and toilet and the discoveries of black insects in plastic bags of dirt.

After nine months, the patient passed away. "But he had good times with his wife and that was very good closure for all of us," Yap shared. "I learnt a lot from this about the resources needed from community and how to ensure a continuity of care from hospital to home."

Xinhui (*left*) might still be relatively inexperienced in palliative care, however, she knows that even though the journey ahead will not be easy, God has shown Himself faithful. "Good or bad or tough, God brought me to it, so He will bring me through it." Photo courtesy of Xinhui Ng.

NOT JUST A WAITING GAME

Well-meaning friends had cautioned Ng about the emotional toll that came with the job.

But during her time as a ward nurse, Ng says she has seen "too many" patients who have passed on that she wishes could have been referred for palliative care earlier. When doctors say treatment options are "limited", it is not the end of the world.

"If we are able to help them – achieve certain goals or allay the anxiety of their caregivers, these are positives. We are there to journey with them."

It is not about "waiting to die", she pointed out. "Life is very, very short – and I don't say that lightly. Since all of us will die one day, we should focus on what we can do to have a better quality of life in the time that we have."

> "In situations like this, it is the Holy Spirit who prompts me. If not, sometimes, it is too overwhelming."

However, the reality of death, pain and symptom-induced suffering that patients face means that they often look for some spiritual support with common questions that arise like, "Why me?"

"I cannot answer that," said Yap. "But they already have the answers, and it is just a matter of how to approach it and draw out the concerns or issues they have."

Addressing patients' psychosocial needs is a skill that Ng is still working on: "Each person reacts differently so you have to convey the message to them in individual ways."

It is important to listen and to facilitate this talk because there is a lot that can be done to help them. "But I can never be over-prepared for such discussions," she said, adding that she always prays before each conversation because sometimes there are situations that"go beyond our imagination".

"When I walk into situations like this, it is God who is guiding me. The Holy Spirit prompts me – if not sometimes, it is just too overwhelming. I have to be very sensitive to His leading so that I can help the person at that moment."

IN HIM AND THROUGH HIM

That guidance also extends to Ng's circuitous route into the field of palliative care.

"God has His ways to lead," said Ng. "There was a period I feared that God would take someone away from me again, but down the road, I think the message from God was more that He just wants us to depend on Him, and to do so wholly.

"Good or bad or tough, God brought me to it, so He will bring me through it."

It is a "simple" faith that Yap holds to. After each patient passes on, Yap gives herself space to find closure with her husband, her team or even her mentors.

There is one particular emotion that has kept her in this field for over 22 years.

"Joy is an important part of my role," Yap said. "Without it, it would be difficult to bring hope to my patients and my team of caregivers."

But she recognises that God holds her centre and it is His joy that she receives each day. "God is my strength. Without Him, I cannot do this for the long haul," she said.

◆ **Text by Tan Huey Ying & Anna Cheang**

Work

Preserving the aroma of Christ: The secret behind Chek Hup's coffee

Joseph Tan with The Blue Sky Choir. The choir was performing at a concert that Chek Hup sponsored in support of World Vision Malaysia. Photo courtesy of World Vision, Malaysia.

Joseph Tan's faith saturates his life. He heads Chek Hup, a company famous for its instant coffee. To Tan, the acronym c.o.f.f.e.e. stands for "Christ Offers Forgiveness For Everyone Everywhere".

"I want the aroma of Christ in the coffee we sell," quips the youthful looking Managing Director.

The verse, Matthew 6:33, is also a compelling motivation that drives him to always put God first, knowing that He will take care of the rest.

Chek Hup was awarded The Brand Laureate SMEs Best Brands Signature Award 2014. Picture from company's website.

BEYOND 7,200 TONNES

Today, Chek Hup, the Malaysian home brand established by Tan's dad in the mid 1900s has a yearly turnover of about RM100 million. The award-winning company produces 7,200 tonnes of instant beverages and rock sugar annually. Its products are stocked in supermarket shelves all across Southeast Asia and Greater China.

Despite the company's success, Tan is mindful of the debt of gratitude to God for the "blessing that has exceeded our wildest dream." As the family business grew, so did his realisation that God's blessings are not meant for selfish pleasure but as a resource for His kingdom.

"We value lives of our staff, we look for their strengths and put them where they can flourish."

This revelation became a conviction in 2014.

While he was preparing his eulogy for his father's funeral, Tan came across a verse in the Bible which said: "In the same way, let your light shine before others, so that they may see your good works and give glory to your Father who is in heaven." (Matthew 5:16) It impressed on him to let God's light shine through the company's good deeds and to glorify Father God in heaven..

The following year, at the company's 50th anniversary, he announced that the company would start contributing 1% of its

Joseph Tan, on the extreme right, next to Malaysian singer Adira at Chek Hup's launch in Kuala Lumpur in 2015.

Chek Hup Coffee had a special mention in local media. Picture from company's website.

annual profit to charitable and Kingdom work, and to increase the contribution by 1% every year until it hits 10%.

Since then, the company has tied up with Christian organisations such as World Vision to help the needy and build God's kingdom.

PEOPLE DRIVEN

At Chek Hup, the staff's personal development and well-being are big on the company's agenda, and this is spelled out in the company's core value, "We value lives."

"Sometimes, we have staff who do not perform well in their work due to a mismatch in their skills and responsibilities. Instead of letting them go, we identify their strengths and put them where they can flourish with their skills," Tan reveals.

"We don't mind spending more to retrain the staff because when we value life, there's trust, respect and security in the company."

The Managing Director went on to explain that when the staff feel valued and secure, they are inspired to work harder, this in turn drives up profit.

MINISTRY AT WORK

Tan is open about the fact that most of his senior management team are Christians. Therefore, regular prayer meetings in the office are important as Tan and his team commit the business to God. He also intends for the staff to witness the difference when God's presence is in the company.

> "The senior management team regularly prays and commits the business to God."

As a coffee manufacturer, Chek Hup employs many foreign workers from Myanmar, Nepal, Bangladesh and Vietnam. Tan makes sure he does not let up on the opportunity to share the gospel with them.

"We partner with pastors from the various churches. They are involved in our sports ministry on Sunday evenings when we take our migrant workers out for games. During their sports activities, the pastors will connect with them."

WISDOM FOR CHALLENGES

When asked what challenges he faces in the coffee business, Tan admitted that it is hard to balance profit and quality. A good bottom line is necessary to remunerate his staff well and yet, the quality of his products is something he cannot compromise on.

Chek Hup's Managing Director, Joseph Tan, with his wife and two sons on a recent holiday. Photo courtesy of Joseph Tan.

It is a fine line to toe and Tan daily turns to God for wisdom to make decisions that have repercussions on his staff.

> "The most important legacy I can leave for my sons is God's Word."

Meanwhile, he is also working on plans to develop a coffee tourism showcase in his factory in Ipoh, Malaysia.

FAMILY FIRST

Despite his hectic work life, Tan makes it a priority to spend time with his wife and two sons, aged nine and 12. "You know, the most important legacy I can leave my sons is God's Word. When they know God's Word, they can stand firmly and seek His path for themselves.

"We try to have family devotions several times a week, where we read the Bible and I share with them my experiences based on the Scripture.

"We need God's Word to guide us on the path that pleases Him."

◆**Text by Ong Juat Heng**

Work

Desi Trisnawati: Helping others succeed was part of her *MasterChef Indonesia* victory

Contestants started calling Desi "mum" after they saw how she carried herself with integrity during the competition, and how she helped guide them. All photos courtesy of Desi Trisnawati.

Reality TV can be harsh, often shining the spotlight on the worst of human nature – the bad, idle, vengeful and selfish. Despite knowing this, hotel director Desi Trisnawati decided to put her cooking chops to the test, signing up as a contestant for Season 2 of *MasterChef Indonesia*, a competitive cooking reality show featuring amateur home cooks.

It was not a decision that was taken lightly.

She had three young children to care for – they were then just seven, eight and 11 – and a family business to run. Going on the show would separate her from them for five months, with no contact at all in the first month.

But after much prayer together with her husband, Mail Chen, they decided to go ahead.

The road to winning Season 2 of *MasterChef Indonesia* was not easy but Desi found her faith growing and doors opening for her to share Kingdom values with others.

"I was surprised because I had always thought that I was not going to win," revealed Desi, now 46, who beat thousands of contestants to take the trophy.

Hailing from Bangka, a small town in the east of Sumatra, the odds were stacked against her.

A SUITCASE FULL OF RECIPES

With just over 300,000 people residing in her hometown, it is nowhere close to being as vibrant as Jakarta. This meant that Desi had limited knowledge about produce from other parts of Indonesia.

To prepare herself, she began practising the MasterChef timed challenges at home. She likened it to a soldier undergoing military training.

"If I go into a war without preparation, I'm dead. I didn't know whether I was going to be chosen … but I imagined myself as if I was in the competition already," she shared.

She took copious notes during her time of preparation, detailing the things she could do with different ingredients in the time limits that she had to work with.

She eventually made it to West Jakarta, where the competition would be filmed, with a suitcase full of recipes.

"Because I came from a small town, my knowledge about food was very limited. Knowing that, I filled the gap with other knowledge."

(*Left to right*) Desi with her husband, Mail, and their three children, Dianne, Reuben and Jason, at a recent family holiday. It was hard for Desi to be away from her family during the competition but her supportive husband and cell group helped to make the journey easier.

That knowledge went on to serve her well, clocking her multiple wins in the first 10 episodes.

It became too predictable, which made for bad TV.

TURNING THE COMPETITION ON ITS HEAD

Worried the show's ratings would decline, the producers met with the contestants and challenged them to step up their game.

During this time, God dropped two words into her heart: "Position yourself."

> "When you build people up, you will be built up as well."

Puzzled, Desi asked God what that meant. He replied: "If you are a producer, what kind of TV show do you want to see? As a contestant, what do you want? If you are a friend, what do you want?"

At once, she understood what God was telling her to do.

After the producers left, she spoke to her competitors and told them plainly: "The success or failure of the show depends on you and me. How do you want to be remembered?"

She then recalled what her spiritual mentor, Samiton Pangellah, told her before she joined the competition: "When you build people up, you will be built up as well."

Desi recently opened a cooking club in her hometown of Bangka. She hopes to inspire and empower the local community by sharing her culinary knowledge.

Suddenly, it all clicked.

"I can see what's lacking in you and me. Can you improve in this area? Can you help me improve in that area?" she asked her competitors.

Instead of making use of their weaknesses to her advantage, she acted on her mentor's advice and helped them to improve their skills in the kitchen.

"Honestly, I was a bit worried. If they improved, I could get eliminated. It wasn't easy but I just clung onto Romans 14:19 in God's word," recalled Desi.

In spite of all that, there were some who did not play fair and even spread rumours about her.

PLAYING FAIR

"I was a bit shocked … there were a lot of people who wanted to win in any way they could," she said.

Every time something unpleasant happened, she recalled her favourite verse from Proverbs 4:23 (NIV): "Above all else, guard your heart, for everything you do flows from it."

As Desi meditated on the verse, she realised that emotions are powerful and, if left unchecked, could destroy a person.

But soon, the long hours of filming – they sometimes pulled 20-hour days – added to the pressure and her emotions began to get the better of her.

One of the biggest lessons that Desi learned during her time at *MasterChef Indonesia* was not to dwell on negative thoughts but to meditate on the truth found in God's Word. She frequently speaks at churches around Indonesia, sharing her testimony.

She began to buy into the rumours swirling around her. One of them, which she later discovered to be untrue, was that she was slated to be eliminated because the judges never liked her.

Then in the top seven, she thought: "This isn't fair. Why am I trying so hard to serve as an example?

> "The Cross wasn't fair either, but it won."

"'My purpose is not to win; it is to leave a legacy for my children. Winning or losing doesn't matter but if I'm going to lose in an unfair way, I'd better leave now."

She contemplated quitting by deliberately presenting bad dishes during the competition's elimination stage. Her husband and cell group members tried to dissuade her to no avail.

But the words of her mentor woke her up.

"Desi, the Cross wasn't fair either," he reminded her. "But it won."

FORCE FOR GOOD

She realised that the issue was not about fairness but obedience. She decided to grit her teeth and do her best, regardless of the situation.

"I thought I was never going to win because I believed that rumour to be true." She even congratulated the runner-up ahead of the results, convinced he was going to take the top spot.

When the judges announced live on October 28, 2012, that she was the winner, she was shocked.

"Thank God! Not because I won, but because He showed me that the negative thoughts in my mind, which I thought were true, were not reality. I was seeing only one side of the story," said Desi.

As she looked back on her MasterChef journey, she recounted how it has helped her faith to grow and how her decision to honour God through her words and deeds has brought blessings.

"For me, the marketplace is another sphere of influence, which is why some people call me a food evangelist!"

"Doing the right thing is the easiest way to show our faith," she said, sharing that even the judges noticed her faith. Her Christian witness also opened doors for her to pray with other contestants of different faiths.

Today, Desi is a sought-after speaker, cook show host and food consultant. She seeks out every opportunity to impart kingdom values to those she crosses paths with.

Today, Desi continues to use her fame and influence for God. She runs cooking classes and is also a food consultant who mentors others like stay-home mums who run small food businesses and restaurants.

"For me, the marketplace is another sphere of influence (John 4:35), which is why some people call me a food evangelist!" she said with a laugh.

"God continues to open doors for me to meet people from different religions because of my profession. So any chance for me to share Kingdom values, I share them!"

◆ **Text by Geraldine Tan**

Work

Banking head honcho went on to work with villagers and ex-convicts

Alex with his wife Channy and children on holiday. Photo by Alex Tee.

He speaks deliberately, his words measured, pausing often to weigh his thoughts.

At 39 going on 40, Alex Tee could have been at the proverbial epitome of his career in the heady world of banking and finance.

This is where the script changes.

TIDE TURNED

Last year he left his job as Managing Director and the Chief Executive of Bank of America, Singapore.

Tee did not just walk away from his job, he walked away from the banking industry altogether, leaving his high finance career well behind him.

> "I really wanted the stewardship to start now ... not when my best years are behind me."

It's a radical move in a world consumed by the money chase. For Tee, this about-turn began with a conversation about five years ago.

"Isaiah 61 distinguishes between prisoners and captives. I asked the Lord: 'What's the difference? Both need to be freed.'

"And the Lord said: 'The captives are people like you who, because of that financial security, would not step out. And all the time, you know that this is not really *life* but you still continue clipping these fat, chunky financial coupons.'"

That set his mind thinking, but he put the conversation on the back burner.

Tee's siblings together with their spouses and mum (*centre back*). Jimmy, on the extreme right, is the youngest and practising to be a surgeon. Without Tee's season in banking, the family wouldn't have had the means to put him through medical school.

Though it was shelved, it was never forgotten.

Tee came to Singapore as a pre-teen to further his education.

His father's business was doing well in Banting, a small town about 45 minutes drive from the capital city of Kuala Lumpur, Malaysia.

The family sent the eldest child down south to Singapore for a better start in life. However, within a couple of years, his parent's business failed and chalked up debts.

By then, Tee was awarded an ASEAN Scholarship, but the money situation remained tight, right up to university.

That episode left an indelible mark on Tee.

SETTING THE HOUSE IN ORDER

So leaving a successful financial career was no light decision – there were also present needs he was already committed to.

As the eldest of five children, Tee helped to finance his younger siblings' education and was also shouldering some of the financial burden of his extended family.

At the same time, he was just starting a family of his own and there were provisions to be made.

"What really touched me is Luke 9:23-24 – those who lose their life will gain it."

"I needed to acquire financial authority fairly quickly, I saw the whole season in banking as God's providence, to open up this span of time to help me do so."

That season of preparation also gave him time to have more conversations with the Lord about his work situation: "It's the time of secret prayer that Jesus calls for, really growing deep and having a real joy to commune with the Lord. That place has granted me a lot of peace."

Just when he was planning his exit, Tee got promoted to the position of Managing Director of Bank of America, Singapore.

POVERTY OF PURPOSE

However, his heart was set on obedience to His call.

"Using the Bible as reference, I recognised that even if I succeeded wildly and went on to head Asia, I would have succeeded at the wrong thing. I didn't want to realise this only at 50 or 60 years old, when my best years are behind me. I really wanted the stewardship to start now.

> "I no longer have that constant nagging sense that the work of these hands will not matter for eternity."

"What also really got me to make the switch is the recognition that, in banking, there is an appearance of flourishing. Even though you are financially abundant, there may be a poverty of purpose. People who have been in it long enough may recognise that."

Tee (*extreme right*) and his team when the office moved to a spanking new building at OUE Bayfront.

Even so, not many make the move.

In the realm of high finance, taking risks and moving into new investment positions are daily assignments for bankers.

The irony is, when risk becomes a personal affair, many turn averse and rather not venture or wager. Perhaps, the smell of certain money and success is too intoxicating.

KINGDOM PURPOSED

Tee, who had spent more than a decade climbing the ladder in high finance, gave it all away for a smaller investment portfolio.

He took on the role of Chief Operating Officer at Garden Impact, an investment company which backs small enterprises that provide jobs mostly for the poor and the marginalised. Tee has since left

Garden Impact Investments and is now a homeschooling father who continues to make direct investments into companies using market solutions to alleviate poverty.

It focuses not only on the financial bottomline, but the well-being of the community as well.

"God's heart is for the poor and people who cannot help themselves. These communities simply need to be connected to the value chains. Without somebody coming in to link them into those chains, they have very little hope.

"Our utmost wish and dream is to be able to fulfil the Great Commission (Matthew 28:16-20) by obeying the Great Commandment to love our neighbour (Matthew 22:36-40)."

Instead of hobnobbing with clients in swanky restaurants, Tee now meets entrepreneurs in sweaty, regional, far-flung places to help them scale up their operations and provide for communities with needs.

"Sacrifices, servanthood, the abundant life – if they are not embodied, there is a risk they remain abstract."

Tee's face lights up when he talks about the different projects he is working on: "I really love to create flourishing communities and see people succeed. If we talk about flourishing communities, that's another way of saying 'the abundant life'."

It is but early days yet for Tee and his career change of less than a year. His family has had to to live more simply on his current, more modest income. When asked if there was even a chance he'd consider returning to the high-octane world of finance – it was a resounding 'No' for an answer.

"No chance," he says firmly.

"You are right that it is a radical shift. For example, the salary I am on now is sort of a rounding error compared to what I used to be on. But I no longer have that constant nagging sense that the work of these hands will not matter for eternity.

On holiday with his wife, Channy, and children, Eli, Emin and Ena.

"If the Bible is the sole authority of how we must live our lives then I'm not going back. What really touched me is Luke 9:23-24 – those who try to save their life will lose it and those who lose their life will gain it."

PUTTING FAITH TO WORK

Tee is also part of the new breed of younger fathers realigning their lives and values to a higher purpose – not just for themselves, but the next generation as well.

"The biggest reason, and a lot of it, is modelling for the children. They need to know what daddy does. I love to bring home these conversations and tell them about the businesses that we invest in. I love to bring them along the journey; I think that's the only way to develop empathy for people.

"Many values that we talk about – sacrifices, servanthood and the abundant life – if they are not embodied, there is always the risk that they just remain in their theological realm … abstract.

"My hope is that the Lord will use all of this – five loaves and two fish – and inspire others who are captive in the industry, battling that poverty of purpose, to simply walk out and seek a life that is really life."

◆Text by Karen Tan

Work

One man's crisis led to jobs for thousands

Image by Rubén Bagüés/Unsplash.com

Mason Tan was a man in crisis. He was the one who brought fast food chain Carl's Jr to the shores of Singapore and Malaysia in 2003. Business took off and by 2008, there were 12 Carl's Jr outlets in Singapore and Malaysia.

Buffeted by its success, Tan partnered the BreadTalk group and entered the China market in 2007. Beijing was hosting the Olympics in 2008 and they wanted to ride on the wave to enter the market with a big bang.

The big bang did come, but not in the way he had envisioned. In 2008, the global financial crisis struck and his joint venture with BreadTalk was hit.

Apart from facing strong financial headwinds, Tan felt pressured by the business culture in China. In order to secure a prime spot for his fast food outlets in shopping malls, he had to entertain business clients, sometimes at karaoke and drinking sessions which were thinly disguised platforms for womanising.

"Something which is right is still right when nobody is doing it and wrong is wrong even if everyone is doing it," said Tan, 54, who became a Christian when he was 36 years old.

He was anxious to deliver results to please his board members, shareholders and vendors.

Though he considered himself just a "Sunday Christian" then, he valued the Sabbath and made it a point to visit church every Sunday in China. That in itself was a major commitment, because in the food and beverage retail sector, up to 40% of the weekly revenue rolled in on weekends.

Tan knew he needed to anchor himself in God – it was a trying time to kick start a new business venture in China and he hardly saw his family, who were residing in Singapore.

The last straw came when a senior director called him to resolve some operational issues in the middle of a Christmas service he was attending in Shanghai, China, where Christmas is not a public holiday.

At that moment, he realised he was compromising too much for the sake of the business and began looking for a successor to take over his role.

Due to 2008 Lehman Brothers financial crisis, the business had to take further hits which cost the business venture millions of dollars. The setback threw him into a brief period of depression as he felt personally accountable for the losses he had to bear.

Packing his bags, he returned to Singapore in 2010. By then, he was 45 years old and he did not know whether there could be a reset button for his life.

Through our work, we want to address not only economic poverty, but also spiritual and emotional poverty.

"Upon reflection, I realised there is no perfect time to serve God, even in the midst of personal financial struggle," he said.

For the following two years, he took a sabbatical leave from full time work and sought the Lord. He prayed, pored over the Bible, attended courses to identify his strengths and reread books such as Rick Warren's *Purpose Driven Life* and Bob Buford's book *Halftime: Moving from Success to Significance*. During this time, he took on ad-hoc job stints, such as being a venture partner in a private equity firm.

"In this period of soul searching, I felt God impressing upon me that I could run a fund to invest in people and businesses and help them to grow. My passion then became helping others realise their dreams," said Tan.

With the support of Dato Dr Kim Tan, a leading social entrepreneur, he set up Garden Impact Investments in 2013.

"God created the garden of Eden for mankind to find love, peace and joy but Adam's sin broke that harmony and poverty resulted," said Tan.

"Through the nature of our work, we want to address not only economic poverty, but also spiritual and emotional poverty."

Garden Impact Investments is a private Singapore-based impact investment holding company. It invests in businesses that create jobs and provide services and products for the poor and marginalised. In addition to financial returns, each investment is monitored for its social impact returns.

Mason Tan (*left*) visiting local villagers in Indonesia to understand their needs for home-based toilets as opposed to communal toilets

Affordable sanitation project in East Java

In Indonesia, Garden Impact invested in Paloma Shopway, a leading mail ordering catalogue business that hired more than 45,000 home-based women and single mothers to be its sales agents. More than 80% of the business were generated outside the Java island. These women collected orders from people in their rural villages, ordered products via their mobile phones and received a commission when the products were shipped.

Also in Indonesia, Garden Impact invested in an affordable funeral services provider which worked with insurance providers to provide a low-cost death and bereavement insurance scheme for needy families. This means that those who could not afford to pay for a funeral for their loved ones need not borrow from loan sharks, which charged exorbitant interest rates, or wait for at least two weeks for other insurers to disburse the money. They could hold the bereavement services immediately.

In Singapore, Garden Impact made an early stage investment in Agape Connecting People, which employed sentence serving prisoners, ex-offenders, delinquent youth and socially displaced persons to provide transportation and call centre services.

So far, Garden Impact has invested approximately S$3.5 million in 10 projects in Singapore, Malaysia, Thailand and Indonesia.

The focus of such social impact investing is not in maximising profits, but impact. Besides creating jobs for the vulnerable, the Key Performance Indicators (KPIs) include providing decent housing to employees and ensuring that their dependents have access to quality tertiary education.

"Regarding financial sustainability, it is enough if the projects generate 5% annualised returns, even though the norm for other traditional venture capitalists is above 30%," said Tan, its chief executive.

"But God does bless and multiply resources."

He believes in a company culture that adopts humility and simplicity. There is no company car policy and all work flights are by budget airlines.

From being merely a "pew-warmer" in church on Sundays, he now tries hard to be a full time follower of Christ in the marketplace from Monday to Saturday. Spending time to study the Bible and daily prayers had become a non-negotiable fixture in his life.

Said Tan: "I hope to do this meaningful work for the rest of my life. The Bible always reminds us our days are numbered. Thus it is important for us seek to honour God by honouring and loving those whom God loved — the poor and the weak."

◆**Text by Janice Tai**

About the writers

Juleen Shaw

Salt&Light Managing Editor Juleen hails from the newsrooms of Singapore Press Holdings and MediaCorp Publishing. Her favourite part of the job is seeing epiphany light up the eyes of interviewees as they recall the moment God became real in their lives.

Tan Huey Ying

Huey Ying is now an Assignments Editor at *Salt&Light*, having worked in finance, events management and swimming industries. She usually has more questions than answers but is always happiest in the water, where she's learning what it means to "be still".

Karen Tan

Karen was a producer at Asia Business News (Singapore), Bloomberg News and CNBC Asia. She subsequently joined the Far East Organisation to oversee corporate social responsibility. Karen was Associate Editor at *Salt&Light*.

Emilyn Tan

Emilyn once spent morning, noon and night in a newsroom in the US, and in MediaCorp Singapore. She gave it up to spend morning, noon and night at home, in the hope that someday she'd have an epiphany of God with His hands in the suds, washing the dishes too.

Rachel Phua

Rachel Phua contributes to *Salt&Light*, where she was formerly a full-time writer. Her stories have also been carried by several US publications, including the Dallas Morning News, the Austin American-Statesman, and the Austin Business Journal.

Geraldine Tan

Geraldine is a former journalist, public relations practitioner and research editor with a penchant for puns, punctuation and a positive attitude. She is always up for the next new adventure. Geraldine was Assistant Editor at *Salt&Light*.

Gracia Lee

Gracia is a journalism graduate who thoroughly enjoys people and words. Thankfully, she gets a satisfying dose of both as a Writer at *Salt&Light*. When she's not working, you will probably find her admiring nature or playing Monopoly Deal with her little brother.

Jane Lee

Jane has been telling stories across Asia, whether as a journalist, a missionary or a brand storyteller, always trying to give the voiceless (and boring) a voice.

Gemma Koh

Gemma has written about everything from spas to scuba diving holidays. But she has a soft spot for telling the stories of lives changed, and of people making a difference. Gemma is a Senior Writer & Copy Editor at *Salt&Light*.

Christine Leow

Christine believes there is always a story waiting to be told. This led to a career scripting and producing news, documentaries and current affairs programmes in MediaCorp News. Christine is now a Senior Writer at *Salt&Light*.

Janice Tai

Salt&Light Senior Writer Janice is a former news correspondent who enjoys immersing herself in: 1) stories of the unseen, unheard and marginalised, 2) the River of Life, and 3) a refreshing pool in the midday heat of Singapore.

Ong Juat Heng

Juat Heng was a journalist in *The Star* before branching out to public relations consultancy and advertising copywriting. As a mother to three adult boys, her chief prayer has always been that they know God intimately.

Dr Tam Wai Jia

A medical doctor, Wai Jia is married to Cliff, whose life of resilience as a cancer survivor inspires her daily. Wai Jia was on the 2016 Forbes 30 under 30 list, one of the Young Outstanding Singaporeans 2011 awardees and is the founder of international non-profit, Kitesong Global.

Felicia Chin

Felicia is a MediaCorp actress who shot to fame in 2003 after emerging as the female champion of *Star Search Singapore*. She has been one of the Top 10 Most Popular Female Artistes in the Star Awards 9 times. She is also an ambassador for World Vision Singapore.

Anna Cheang

Anna is an undergraduate who dreams to give a voice to the voiceless. Having interned at *Salt&Light*, she is one step closer to achieving her dream, even as she meets and learns from many inspiring individuals through this journey

To find more *Salt&Light* stories of faith at work, go to:

Website : http://saltandlight.sg
Facebook : https://www.facebook.com/saltandlight.sg
Instagram : https://www.instagram.com/saltandlight.sg
Telegram : https://t.me/saltandlightsg
Twitter : https://www.twitter.com/saltandlightsg
E-mail : hello@saltandlight.sg